DATE DUE

2√outs to 10/07			
2 Lib			
		DISCARDED	

ANTI-SEMITISM

ANTI-SEMITISM

EDWARD F. DOLAN, JR.

FRANKLIN WATTS 1985
NEW YORK LONDON TORONTO SYDNEY

Photographs courtesy of:
Bettmann Archive: pp. 31, 38, 49;
Zionist Archives: p. 56;
AP/Wide World: pp. 63, 66;
Religious News Services: pp. 71, 100, 123, 124;
Museum of the City of New York: p. 89.

Library of Congress Cataloging in Publication Data

Dolan, Edward F., 1924–
Anti-Semitism.

Bibliography: p
Includes index.
Summary: Examines the origin and development of
antisemitism as well as the effect it has had on the
Jewish people.
1. Antisemitism—History—Juvenile literature.
2. Antisemitism—United States—History—Juvenile
literature. 3. Jews—United States—History—Juvenile
literature. 4. United States—Ethnic relations—
Juvenile literature. [1. Antisemitism—History.
2. Jews—History. 3. Ethnic relations] I. Title.
DS145.D75 1985   305.8'924'073   85-8820
ISBN 0-531-10068-5

CONTENTS

ANTI-
SEMITISM

INTRODUCTION

Prejudice is an ugliness that exists in every part of the world. It is the dislike and the distrust that people feel for others whose ethnic backgrounds, political opinions, religious beliefs, lifestyles, or even physical characteristics are different from their own.

At one time or another virtually every group has felt the sting of someone else's prejudice. Among the people who have suffered that sting most deeply and for the longest time are the Jews. The hate that has been directed toward them is now two thousand years old—and may even date back as far as four thousand years. It has come to be known as anti-Semitism. The term is derived from the fact that the Jews are members of the population group known as Semites.

In this book, we're going to take a close look at all aspects of anti-Semitism. We'll see the various ideas that give it life. We'll see how those ideas took shape long ago. We'll see what they have done through the centuries—the discomfort, heartbreak, anguish, injustice, and outright horror that they have brought to the Jewish people. And we'll see what they are doing to Jews across the world today.

In looking at these ideas we'll come upon two very basic facts. First, the attitudes are based, for the most part, on false premises and misunderstandings of Jews—false premises and misunderstandings that might begin to evaporate should one make the effort and take the time to get to know personally the people against whom they are directed. Like the prejudices directed against *any* individual or group, they have little to do with the true nature of their victims.

Second, despite all the problems that today's world faces, a study of history will quickly show us that we live in one of the most enlightened eras that humankind has ever seen. Ours is an age of widespread education, of instant worldwide communication, of magnificent scientific advances, of progress along a varied number of social fronts. We're going to find in this book that most of the ideas behind anti-Semitism were born centuries ago and are known to have sprung from fears, angers, and superstitions, all of which had little or no basis in fact. Yet, as advanced as our era may be, far too many people cling to these old and groundless ideas. They have been passed down from generation to generation and people have accepted them without thinking about them, without testing to find if they are false.

In all, this willingness to accept blindly an ancient ugliness and not put it to the acid test of question in an age of widespread accomplishment and learning is one of the strangest facts about modern life. It simply proves one long-established truth: Prejudice is a deep-seated human trait. History leaves no doubt that the fears and angers we feel for someone different from ourselves have been with us since the dawn of time. It is a trait so deep-seated that it might well remain in us to the end of time.

And this brings us to the purpose of this book. It is simply, by telling the story of what has been done to one people, to point up the danger and foolishness of prejudice of *any* kind. Hopefully, then, we can take steps to rid our own lives of this ugliest of human traits.

We may never be rid of it completely because it is such an ingrained trait. But the attempt to do so, for our own personal growth and for the peace and happiness of those who share this life with us, is unquestionably more than worth the try.

CHAPTER ONE

A PORTRAIT OF HATRED

Throughout history, people of all ethnic and religious groups have felt the sting of someone's prejudice. They have been scorned perhaps for the color of their skin, the shape of their eyes and noses, their clothing, their beliefs or disbeliefs in God, or their ways of living. They have seen and heard the dislikes expressed in various hostile ways. Perhaps you yourself have personally felt the bite of such angers.

If you're black, have you heard yourself called a nigger, a jig, or a jungle bunny?

If you're of Hispanic origin, how many people have called you a spic or a greaser?

As a black or a Hispanic, how often have you heard your people dismissed as shiftless and lazy? How often have you been told that you and your kind like nothing better than to sleep away your lives?

If you're white, you've likely heard yourself called a honky. You were long ago nicknamed a frog if you're of French descent, a hunkie if you come from a Polish background, or a wop if you're born of an Italian family. If you're an Irish Catholic, how many have said that you're a dumb Mick or a mackerel snapper (from the Catholic tradition of eating fish in place of meat on Fridays)? And, if you're a Catholic of any national origin, you can be sure that someone at some time has said that you're not to be trusted as a citizen because you're more likely to obey the Pope in Rome than the laws of your country.

Today, prejudicial jokes that make cruel fun of nationalities can be heard everywhere: jokes, for example, that characterize the Polish and Italian people as stupid. Such jokes are anything but new.

All the jokes and insulting names are anything but new because prejudice is itself anything but new. It is an ugliness that has likely been with us from the very dawn of time. Throughout history it has served—and today continues to serve—a number of human shortcomings. As we'll see throughout this book, some people have used it to raise their own self-esteem by looking down on others and calling them inferior. Some have used it to give focus to their anger when things have gone wrong in their lives, perhaps saying that they cannot find work because those of another race have taken all the jobs in a certain line of endeavor. Some have used it as a way to explain mysterious happenings for which there were, as yet, no scientific explanations; for instance, in ages past, certain races were accused of starting plagues or carrying particular illnesses. Some political factions have used prejudice to gain strength or to avoid being blamed for the troubles in their countries; they've done so by identifying a scapegoat—by blaming all of a nation's troubles on one or more of the groups living there.

Fortunately, not everyone is prejudiced. Throughout history there have been countless people who have sought to understand, like, and appreciate those of backgrounds and customs different from theirs. But, unfortunately, the prejudiced—far too many of them—have always been around and they have made life everything from an unpleasant experience to an outright torture for the targets of their hate.

Among those who have suffered most at the hands of prejudice are the Jews. Though small in number when compared to other groups, they constitute one of the most significant bodies of people in the world having made great contributions over the centuries to science, medicine, commerce, and the arts. (The exact number of Jews in the world today is difficult to assess because so many have intermarried with other peoples. A recent survey of the Jewish religion, however, showed that worldwide, the Jewish religion has a membership of more than 16 million. In this book we're going to be talking about the angers, the misunderstandings, and the attacks that these people have endured since the earliest days of recorded history.

ANTI-SEMITISM

Anti-Semitism is the term used to designate the prejudice directed against the Jews. Like the prejudice that is leveled against any other group, it serves the many different human shortcomings that were mentioned above. In so doing it takes three forms. Each form can operate alone or can be connected with the others. The three are: personal prejudice, discrimination, and persecution.

The personal prejudice is seen in all the ugly statements and jokes that individuals make. Should you be a Jew, you have probably felt the face-slap of personal prejudice, no matter how young you are. You need not be told that your people have long been viciously nicknamed kikes, hebes, sheenies, and Hymies. If you haven't heard it already, you'll undoubtedly soon hear someone say that your people are too sharp to be trusted in business dealings and that you all stick together, watching out only for each other and caring little about anyone else.

Discrimination is seen in the fact that Jews have often been denied jobs because they are Jews. This was seen in Germany when Adolf Hitler, one of the truly monstrous Jew haters in history, came to power in the early 1930s. Immediately he launched a campaign to ban Jews from positions in teaching, music, the press, and public service. At the same time he took steps to develop in German children a hatred of everything Jewish. For example, he ordered that a storybook titled *Der Gifpilz (The Poisonous Mushroom)* be distributed to all the early grammar school grades. The book contained seventeen stories. All told of how the Jew was a "poisonous mushroom" that threatened civilized people everywhere.

Discrimination has shown its treacherous self in a number of other ways over the centuries. Jews have been prohibited at times from buying homes in gentile (non-Jewish) neighborhoods. They have been denied membership in certain gentile social clubs and organizations. In common with the blacks, there was a time when Jews could not register in certain hotels, go to dinner in certain restaurants, or enjoy relaxing on certain beaches.

Ugly as prejudice and discrimination are, they pale when contrasted with the acts of persecution that have been directed against the Jews at intervals in history. Chiefly responsible for these acts have been governments, political bodies, and religious groups (those of Roman Catholicism and Protestantism among them). As we'll find in the coming chapters, fits of anti-Semitism over political, economic, and religious matters have seen the entire Jewish populations deported at times from such countries as Spain and England.

Undoubtedly, the worst acts of Jewish persecution ever witnessed took place in our own century, when Hitler's Nazis, after conquering much of Europe, set out in the 1940s to exterminate all the Jews living on the Continent. Residing there at the time were between 9 and 10 million Jews. Hitler killed more than 6 million of their number, plus countless others—Poles, Slavs, and Russians among them—whom he had come to despise.

SPECIAL POINTS ABOUT
ANTI-SEMITISM

Here now are some special points that should be remembered as you read the coming chapters.

First, though the Jews have suffered at the hands of various peoples throughout history, the term *anti-Semitism* is a fairly new one. It was invented by a German writer, Wilhelm Marr, in 1879. He dreamed it up while writing an anti-Jewish pamphlet, a booklet in which he accused wealthy Jews of trying to dominate Germany economically. The term may be a new one, but, because the practice of anti-Semitism is very old, we'll be using the word throughout this book, even when talking of those times long before Wilhelm Marr lived.

Second, the term is misleading in its use of the word *Semitism*. Semitism refers to the Semites, a broad group of people who can trace their origins back to the Near East and northern Africa. Their ancestors spoke what are called the Hamito-Semitic languages. Included in the group are Ethiopians, many Arabian peoples, and the Jews. Anti-Semitism, however, refers only to hatred of the Jews and does not include their fellow Semites. The Jews, according to some sources, make up only about 10 to 15 percent of all the Semitic peoples.

Third, anti-Semitism is often said to be a form of racial prejudice. Strictly speaking, this is not true because anthropologists believe that the Jews are not actually a race. As substantiation for this belief, the anthropologists point to studies showing that all Jews do not evidence the same physical characteristics; the studies further reveal that, in time, the Jews almost always reflect the mental and physical characteristics of the peoples among whom they live and with whom they intermarry. Since the Jews are such an old people, it is difficult and confusing to settle on their actual origin. In general, it can only be said that, rather than being a race to themselves, they may have come from an assortment of ethnic groups that spoke a common language and shared a common heritage.

Finally, because it embraces prejudice, discrimination, and persecution, anti-Semitism has two definitions—a strict one and one that is loose and informal. The strict definition regards anti-Semitism as a definite tool employed by governments, rulers, political and social factions, and religious bodies to gain an advantage for themselves by acting against one segment (or several segments) of the population. Such moves tend to unite other parts of the population behind the troublemaker by appealing to their own personal hates. In a nutshell, the group being persecuted or discriminated against is turned into a scapegoat.

Again, Nazi Germany can stand as a horrible example here. When Hitler first entered politics, his country was suffering from terrible economic conditions because of the costs of its defeat in World War I. Further, the German people, once so proud of their military might, were deeply humiliated by the defeat. Hitler gave them a scapegoat on whom they could heap the blame for their plight. Ceaselessly he ranted that Jewish financiers, eager to reap great profits from armament sales, had been chiefly responsible for starting the war. The charges were ridiculous—as anyone who has studied the causes of the war knows—but they drew thousands of Germans to his Nazi party and were instrumental in bringing him at last to power.

The loose definition marks anti-Semitism as a general cultural and personal prejudice toward and discrimination against the Jews. It is under this loose definition that we run into personal prejudice and much discrimination. It is here that we hear Jews called by insulting names, that we hear of them sticking close together and caring little for others, and that we see some landlords refusing to sell or rent them homes in gentile neighborhoods.

And it is under this loose definition that we hear only silence when some unfairness is done to the Jews. For instance, two major international airlines some years ago removed from their advertising all mention of their routes to Israel. The mention was dropped because the airlines allegedly did not want to antagonize potential Arab customers, who have long been upset by the presence of the Jewish state in their midst. The omission constituted an unfairness against the Jews and Israel. But few gentiles spoke out against it, and information about the routes was returned to the advertising only after persistent complaints by American Jewish organizations.

Though the two definitions are separate, they are insidiously connected. It is the assorted cultural and personal prejudices within a country that make it possible for a government or a faction to move against the Jews—or any group—and persecute them, as was the case in Hitler's Germany. Conversely, persecution by a government or a faction can arouse to a fury the personal prejudices felt by a society for some group within it. In all, the two definitions form a vicious circle, with each feeding on the other. As we go along we'll see the two definitions at their work of creating this vicious circle.

THE FACE OF
ANTI-SEMITISM

In great part, prejudice springs from fear: the fear that someone might be better than we are, might take a job we want, might somehow change for the worse our neighborhood, or might challenge our dearest beliefs—and even prove them wrong—with his or her beliefs. It also springs from dislike, the dislike that so many people feel for anyone different from themselves. And, in very great part, prejudice springs from unfamiliarity, from not getting to know the people against whom it is directed and from not taking the trouble to learn about them for ourselves.

No matter what the source of the prejudice is, one of two things can happen when it shows itself. First, it may well disappear, in part or altogether, when we come to know the people whom we've hitherto disliked or feared. Haven't we all heard, or even made, such remarks as "I don't like Jews (or blacks, Hispanics, Catholics, Protestants), but I've gotten to know Saul Greenbaum and I like him very much." Or: "I've always been afraid of gypsies because I've heard they'll steal you blind. But my new friend Christine has gypsy blood and she's as honest as can be."

Second, suppose that our minds are closed. Suppose that we're so stubborn, so fearful of the truth, or so lazy that we refuse to find out about the disliked or feared person. Almost invariably—perhaps knowing deep down inside how wrong we are in failing to act—we begin looking for reasons to justify our prejudice. Color of the skin and other physical characteristics provide the simplest "justifications" of all. It's so easy to say "I don't like those people" because they're black, white, brown, or red or because they have slanted eyes, round eyes, long noses, short noses, thick lips, or thin lips.

The Jews, in common with the blacks, have long suffered from these sorts of justifications. Anti-Semitic books, plays, and drawings have attacked Jews by showing certain physical characteristics: dark skin, dark eyes, sharply defined noses, and a distinctive manner of speech. But the prejudiced have run into problems when using such physical traits as anti-Semitic justifications. This is because, unlike the blacks, the Jews do not seem to be a distinct race and are known to take on the characteristics of the people among whom they live or with whom they intermarry. The result is that many Jews simply do not show any of the above physical characteristics. And so the world's prejudiced people have always had to turn in other directions for their venom. Over the centuries they have invented a whole series of ideas to justify their hatred. Here are the most basic of these ideas:

1. The Jews are taught by their religion that they are "God's Chosen People." As a result, they look on themselves as superior to all other people.

2. The Jews engage in strange, dangerous, and even murderous religious practices.

3. The Jews are a cursed lot, doomed to eternal suffering and deserving of the hatred directed against them because their ancestors crucified Jesus Christ.

4. The Jews are clannish. They stick together and care little about others. In great part, their clannishness comes from their belief that they are "God's Chosen People" and, hence, superior to everyone else.

5. The Jews are too sharp in their business dealings. They are not to be trusted in money matters. Because of this business acumen, most Jews are rich.

6. Rich Jews are greedy and want to dominate the world.

7. The Jews are not to be trusted politically. They are more loyal to themselves and their recently acquired homeland, Israel, than to the countries in which they live.

The list could also contain a number of other ideas, among them several that are contrary to those mentioned above. For instance, although called money-hungry and rich, the Jews have also been accused of being socialists, anarchists, and Communists, all of whom are supposed to scorn the concept of personal wealth.

Harsh and hurtful from beginning to end, the list contains the basic ideas that make anti-Semitism work. All date back over long centuries. We can be thankful that they are not shared by everyone. Fortunately, as was said earlier, prejudice does not extend itself to every last person in the world, and there are millions of people who wish the Jews no harm, who would do them no injustice, and who regard them as close and trusted friends. But there are far too many people who do hold these ideas. Some harbor them all, some just a few, and some just one or two. Regardless of how many or how few are held by any given individual, they prompt three questions that we'll try to answer in the next chapters: When in history did these basic ideas first take shape? Why did they take shape? And how, once born, did they grow and become so strong that they remain in force today?

CHAPTER TWO

THE ROOTS OF A HATRED

To trace anti-Semitism to its very roots we have to travel back four thousand years to a story that contains three elements. Each element served to make the Jews a "people apart" from the rest of the world. It was this apartness that paved the way to the prejudices Jews yet suffer today. The first element had to do with a concept that is very old to us, but one that was brand-new to the ancients, and as radical to them as the ideas of a woman president in the United States is to many people today.

A NEW IDEA

Most of what we know of the earliest days of Jewish history comes from the Bible, especially the Old Testament. Some of that history may be factual, but so much of it is clouded in myth that no one can say where fact begins.

The Jews themselves, so the Bible teaches, are the descendants of the prophet Abraham and are said to have come from the members of a tribe or a number of tribes called by either of two names—the Yehudah or Judah. The term *Jew* is derived from the Latin word *Judaeus* and the Hebrew *Yehudi*. Since the Jews are not thought to be a race, the term today means the followers of the religion Judaism.

Biblical history tells us that four thousand years ago Jewish tribes were living alongside various gentile peoples in the lands at the eastern end of the Mediterranean Sea. They were dry and windswept lands that began at the Tigris and Euphrates rivers in Mesopotamia (now Iraq) and sprawled southwest through where the countries of Syria, Jordan, and Israel today stand. The Jews, who may originally have been a nomadic group from somewhere in Asia, lived off these lands as farmers and shepherds. The gentiles around them tended mainly to commercial business.

Much of the early Jewish population was concentrated in the coastal area where today's state of Israel is to be found. Over the centuries, the area has been known by various names: first, as Canaan and then as Palestine, Judah, Judea, and Israel. The name, Canaan, is thought to have meant "land of the purple." It seems to have come from a well-known dye produced there.

In their earliest days the Jews differed little from their gentile neighbors. Like the gentiles, they were pagans, worshiping a collection of gods that governed all aspects of daily life. But, about 2000 B.C., a respected thinker living in their midst— Abraham—challenged their pagan ways and altered their religious history for all time to come.

He preached that there were not many gods but just one. Claiming to have met this God, Abraham called Him Jehovah (though no one knows for certain, the name was probably pronounced "Yahweh" because it was spelled with the sacred Jewish letters YHWH) and said that He was the only true God. Abraham went on to say that Jehovah had promised to make the Jews his "Chosen People" and would watch over them if they worshiped Him and spread His word.

The Jews accepted Abraham's teachings and became one of the first people in antiquity—perhaps the first—to embrace monotheism, the concept of a single Deity. (Other early people had come close to monotheism by having a single god who was major to all their other gods.) In this way, the religion of Judaism was born and the first of the three elements that set the Jews apart from all other people was created. For the first time a doorway was opened on the Jews, leading to the antagonism that so many individuals have always felt for anyone who dares to be "different" and not think as they think.

THE TURBULENT YEARS

The doorway was not, however, to swing wide open for many years. In the meantime, the second element put in an appearance. It set the Jews even further apart from the rest of the world. Here is what happened.

Because of various problems, the Jews left their homeland three times in the next centuries and went to live in other countries. They were usually first welcomed. Later they grew to be despised as outsiders with, so the people felt, strange and even dangerous religious, personal, and business habits.

Their first departure came in about 1600 B.C. when famine ravaged great areas of their land. A number of Jewish tribes moved southwest into Egypt in search of food. Welcomed there, they remained in Egypt for close to four hundred years. At first, they lived freely as shepherds, but were eventually, with the coming to power of tyrannical pharaohs, reduced to slavery. The Egyptian stay ended when the tribes, led by Moses, escaped back to Canaan, conquered the people there, and established a kingdom that prospered for years under such men as David and Saul.

The next departure came after tribal disputes led to the division of the kingdom into two realms: Israel and Judah. Both met with the disaster of invasion. Israel fell to the Assyrians while Judah, in 586 B.C., was seized by one of the major powers of the day—the Babylonian nation of the Mesopotamian area.

Israel disappeared beneath the heel of its conqueror. But not the people of Judah. Fighting a series of bloody battles—one of which destroyed their major city, Jerusalem—they rebelled against

An early eighteenth-century woodcut showing Abraham, the Jewish patriarch, leading his people into the land of Canaan. Abraham believed that there was only one God and the Jews were his Chosen People, thus setting them apart from their pagan neighbors.

[17]

their Babylonian masters. But, in the end, they were defeated. It was this defeat that brought about the second departure. The Babylonians, wanting no further trouble with the rebels, exiled the Jews of Judah to Babylon and held them prisoner there.

The Babylonian captivity lasted for forty-eight years, ending when the Persians conquered the nation in 539 B.C. The Jews were permitted to return home, only to face centuries more of strife. In turn, their land fell to the Greeks, the Egyptians, and the Syrians, at last becoming an outpost of the Roman Empire in 63 B.C. The early years of Roman rule saw Jesus of Nazareth appear with the simple philosophy that became Christianity.

And the Roman years gave impetus to the third and final departure from the homeland. In what is known in Jewish history as the Diaspora (from the Greek word meaning "dispersion"), the Jews left to settle in all parts of the then-known world: in the Arab lands, in Asia, in Africa, and in Europe. They departed after twice rebelling against their Roman masters in the years following Jesus Christ's death. The Romans quelled both uprisings, smashed the nation, and threatened to obliterate the Jewish religion. The Jews felt that they must leave to safeguard their lives and preserve their religious beliefs. (Though the departures were many in the Roman years, the Diaspora actually began at a much earlier date—at the time of the Babylonian Captivity. This will be explained in Chapter 3.)

Three times the Jews had left their homeland. They seemed destined to be the nomads that they had originally been. Now they were to be away for centuries, a displaced people often scorned, feared, hated, and exploited because they were aliens in the lands in which they settled.

THE THIRD ELEMENT

The third element in the early Jewish story is first seen in the years of the Babylonian exile. It took shape because the Jews were well treated while held in captivity.

The Babylonian government was an enlightened one. It allowed the prisoners to blend into the society, even going so far as to build houses for them. Permitted to live freely, the Jews prospered. Many had brought much wealth—gold and jewels— from home and they now put it to use, establishing themselves as bankers and merchants. They also proved themselves to be first-class traders.

Babylon was centrally located in the ancient world. From it, overland trade routes stretched away to countries both near and far. The Jews used their wealth to dispatch caravans along these routes. Soon they were trading with lands as distant as China, and growing wealthier and wealthier with each shipment. When the exile ended, many Jews chose to remain in Babylon and continue running their profitable businesses.

Born in the Babylonian exile was the reputation that the Jews are good businessmen. It was a reputation that, for reasons we'll see in coming chapters, was to grow and become twisted through the centuries. In time, the Jews were to be seen not only as good, but shrewd and wily businessmen. They were to be seen as untrustworthy in money dealings, with virtually all of their number thought to be rich because of their commercial know-how. But, as we'll also see in the coming chapters, the Jews are just like other people in economic matters. They have always done well in any country where they have been permitted to attend school, obtain work, and blend in with the rest of the population. As is true of other peoples, some of their number have been exceptionally good businessmen and *some have not*. In all, the idea that Jews are naturally shrewd businessmen—and rich as a result—has long been proven to be a myth.

As a case in point we need only look again at Nazi Germany. In his speeches, remember, Hitler claimed that Jewish financiers were responsible for triggering World War I, at the same time indicating that vast numbers of German Jews were rich. The fact of the matter was that most Jews in Germany at the time were small businessmen and shopkeepers.

But, no matter that it be myth and no matter that other people have done equally well in business, this reputation has haunted the Jews throughout the centuries and has caused them trouble wherever they have gone.

THREE ROOTS OF HATRED

The three elements—a religion different from those around it, a people fated to live for centuries as strangers in other countries, and the reputation of being too shrewd in business practices—served as the roots of the twisted and vile plant that would one day be called anti-Semitism. Out of these very basic roots have come all the different prejudices and hates that the world has seen directed against the Jews for centuries.

It's time now to see the cruelty and heartbreak that each root has produced. We'll start with the oldest and deepest root of all.

CHAPTER THREE

THE DEEPEST ROOT

Judaism, the Jewish religion, provided anti-Semitism with its oldest and deepest root. The Jews did more than set themselves apart from the pagans of antiquity when they embraced monotheism, the worship of a single Deity. They went on remaining apart when, centuries later, monotheism swept great parts of the world and saw paganism replaced by Christianity in Europe and by Islam in the Arabian countries.

Why did the Jews continue to remain a people apart from their fellow single-God believers? For the very same reasons that the Islamics and Christians isolated themselves from each other. Each of these three religions thought that its God was the true God. Each cherished its own rites, practices, and beliefs. Each, then, shunned and too often hated the other. The same held true when a second Christian religion—Protestantism—later came into being. It was a situation that has, in many parts of the world, persisted to this day.

THE EARLIEST DIFFERENCES

It is possible that there was some anti-Semitism in the earliest days of Jewish history. The Jews, you'll remember, worked their homeland as small farmers and shepherds. Their gentile neighbors lived in the cities and tended to commerce and trade. Very likely the gentiles felt a contempt for the Jews—the sort of contempt that many city dwellers today feel for rural people and that is reflected in such names as "yokels" and "rubes." And, very likely, as is true of many rural people today, the Jews felt a similar contempt for the city dwellers.

If there was any prejudice at all, historians believe that it was slight and inconsequential. In general, the Jews and gentiles of antiquity got along well and mingled together without undue friction. The first genuine trouble cropped up sometime after the establishment of Judaism and had to do with a number of the beliefs being developed by the Jews. (Many historians believe that this trouble cannot actually be classified as anti-Semitism because it did not contain all the elements that in later centuries came to be identified with anti-Semitism—among them the hatred of physical characteristics and the idea that the Jews were a cursed people. But the trouble has to be a part of our story because it did create antagonisms between the Jews and gentiles.)

The trouble centered on the fact that the Jews early endowed Judaism with a number of customs and laws. Many of the laws had to do with diet and prohibited the Jews from eating certain meats (a chief one being pork), birds that had no feathers or could not fly, and fish that had no fins or scales. Though the laws—which were based on the writings of Moses—were established as religious precepts, they may well have been grounded in ancient Jewish ideas of good health. Perhaps the Jews had noticed that illness at times followed the eating of these foods and decided it best to outlaw them. If so, they certainly had a point in the case of pork. Today we know that pork, when improperly cooked, poses the threat of the disease trichinosis.

Whatever the reason for the dietary laws, they caused the Jews to be sickened by gentile eating habits. To the Jews, the gentiles were "unclean." Consequently, they were to be shunned. There was to be no social traffic with them. And, of course, marriage with a gentile was out of the question.

Understandably, it was not long before the gentiles were seeing the Jews as a people of strange habits who kept to themselves and wanted no part of their neighbors. Popping out here were the first buds of the idea that the Jews are clannish and care for none but themselves.

Next, the gentiles, perhaps in retaliation, began circulating stories that the Jews were actually the unclean ones. The Egyptians, during one period when the Jews were opposing them politically, were responsible for an especially vicious story. It held that the Jews had not escaped from Egypt centuries earlier, but had been banished from the country because they were a leprous group and because Egypt had wanted to purify its temples and people of their presence. The story persisted through the years and ultimately found its way into the writings of several Greek authors.

The Greek writers added a few details of their own. They said the Jews were descended from tribes of lepers, adding that it was the inheritance of leprosy that made them avoid the eating of pork. In the eyes of the writers, swine easily contracted leprosy and just as easily passed it on to any human who was prone to the disease.

And so the stage of anti-Semitism was set for the future. Far worse stories were to come.

THE DIASPORA

As you know, the Diaspora saw the Jews move out in all directions from their homeland. Technically, the Diaspora is said to have begun while the Jews were exiled in Babylon. At that time, remember, they proved themselves first-class traders by sending goods to places as distant as China. To help facilitate the commerce, some Jews settled in towns along the trade routes and in China itself, later remaining behind when the exile ended. The greatest movement in the Diaspora, however, came in the several centuries following the death of Jesus Christ—centuries that saw Christianity rise in the West, and Islam in the East.

In those centuries the Jews settled in the Arabian world and in all parts of the Roman Empire. Actually, it seems that most Jews went first to the countries of the Roman Empire and later to the Arabian areas, where the religion, Islam, was practiced. We'll look first, however, at their experience in the Islamic—or Muslim—regions because it can be more briefly described. In the seventh century A.D., those regions, thanks to Arabian conquests, began to stretch from India through the Middle East and along the shores of North Africa to Spain in Europe.

LIFE IN ISLAM

The Jews were first generally welcomed in the Muslim countries. The welcome was extended for two reasons. First, in part, Islam was an outgrowth of Judaism and so, for a time at least, Judaism was widely respected among the Muslim people. Second, mostly for economic and political reasons, the Muslims of the day had no love for the Christian nations.

(It should be noted here that Islam was also an outgrowth of Christianity. The religion was founded in the seventh century A.D. by Mohammed, a traveling merchant from Mecca, after he encountered a number of Jews and Christians in his journeys and was inspired by their word of a single Deity. He returned home, denounced the worship of idols, and preached the existence of a single God, whom he called Allah. Mohammed was soon revered by his followers as a prophet sent from God. Islam today is practiced by some 400 million people. It is found principally in the Arab countries, in southwest Asia, in northern and eastern Africa, and in such countries as Turkey, Iran, and India.)

Welcomed in the Islamic countries, the Jews thrived just as they had done during the Babylonian capitivity. In fact, many historians look on this time as one of the great periods in Jewish history. As writer Max I. Dimont points out in his book *Jews, God and History,* the Islamic nations saw the Jews become outstanding writers, philosophers, scientists, doctors, tradesmen, financiers, and statesmen.

But, to a great extent, the welcome eventually dissolved into unfriendliness. Trouble came when the Jews stuck to their religious beliefs and stubbornly resisted the efforts of the Muslims to convert them to Islam. Offended, the Muslims took a number of retaliatory steps. In some areas they restricted the Jews to certain neighborhoods. In others, Jews were forced to wear special clothing or badges so that the public could easily avoid their company. And, in some areas, they were required to pay special taxes.

The Islamic nations, at the time the Jews were first living there, were ranked among the most powerful countries on earth. That power was lost around the twelfth century A.D. With its passing came the close of the Jewish "golden age" among the Muslims.

THE EARLY ROMAN
EXPERIENCE

When the Jews began migrating to areas of the Roman Empire, Christ had been but recently crucified. Though Christianity was beginning to make itself widely felt, the empire was still a pagan state.

The pagan Romans accorded the Jews a dual welcome. On the one hand, democratic Roman laws protected their religious rights and allowed them to practice Judaism freely. But, on the other, many Romans shunned the monotheistic Jews as a strange lot with some pretty odd religious views.

In time, however, the laws permitting the Jews to practice their religion caused antagonism in several quarters. It must be said that some Jews may themselves have been at fault for this enmity. At the core of the trouble was the suspicion that, when released from certain civic obligations so that they could observe the Sabbath, many Jews tried to be exempted from other civic duties as well. If this were indeed the case, it was, naturally, a maneuver bound to ignite widespread hostility among the gentiles.

Further, the Jews—as was their right—often took sides in political disputes within the empire. This was especially true in Egypt, where they opposed the aristocratic families who had controlled the nation prior to the coming of Roman might and who wished nothing more than to be returned to power. Here was a political powder keg that, at one point in the first century A.D., exploded in vicious mob attacks of the Jews in the Egyptian city of Alexandria.

Additional problems came from the fact that, for a time in their history, the pagan Romans worshiped their emperors as gods. The Jews, by practicing their own religion, were soon looked upon as snubbing the emperor-gods and thus defying their authority as leaders. Furious at the imagined snubs, the demented emperor Caligula once ordered the Jews to build a statue in his image and then bow down to it. He was assassinated by political rivals before the order was put into effect. There is no telling what trouble might have erupted had he lived long enough to see the Jews, as would surely have been the case, ignore his edict.

In general, however, though suffering anti-Semitic outbreaks periodically and viewed as an odd lot, the Jews fared reasonably well in the pagan empire. But things changed drastically with the arrival of a new Roman era—the era of early Christianity.

THE EARLY CHRISTIAN
EXPERIENCE

In the years following the death of Jesus Christ, Christianity fanned out from his birthplace to the whole of the Roman Empire. Christ's disciples and their followers traveled far afield to preach and establish Christian beliefs and worship. Soon Christian communities were to be found virtually everywhere in the empire. Finally, in A.D. 325, the emperor Constantine the Great decreed Christianity to be the empire's official religion and the Catholic Church to be the empire's official church.

(In time, the Catholic Church divided itself into two branches, with one centered in the Latin-speaking countries to the west, and the other in the Greek-speaking countries to the east. The western branch was the Roman Catholic Church, headquartered at Rome and presided over by the Pope. The Greek-speaking branch became known as the Eastern Church. Its headquarters were in Constantinople [now Istanbul] in what is today Turkey. Out of it grew the family of eastern churches today called the Orthodox churches.)

For two reasons the Jews faced hard times when Christianity won the empire over. First, as the official church of the empire, the Catholic Church felt that everyone within the empire should belong to it. This, of course, was an idea totally unacceptable to the Jews, who held to their beliefs and rejected the Christian concept of Jesus as the Son of God.

Second, the Catholic leadership—because so many pagan Romans had been attracted to Judaism rather than Christianity—looked on Jewry as a political force that could stand in the way of the further spread of their faith. The public angers engendered by these two reasons saw the early Christians, who themselves had once been persecuted by the Roman authorities for their beliefs, now attack the Jews. Jews were beaten in various empire cities. Jewish centers of worship and learning, the synagogues, were often ransacked and burned.

As if things weren't bad enough, matters worsened in the fifth century A.D. That was the century that saw northern barbarian hordes—the Vandals and Visigoths—attack Rome and bring the empire, which had long been tottering because of corruption and internal strife, crashing down. The invaders, soon adopting Christianity, turned a fanatical eye on the Jews and decreed that they, too, must join the faith. In one of the conquered areas—Spain—Judaism was outlawed and the Jews were forcibly baptized as Christians. Baptism through threat and force was seen in many other locales in the next years.

The year A.D. 590, however, marked the beginning of an era of relative peace for the Jews. The man responsible for it was Pope Gregory I. Like all Catholics, he felt the Jews should belong to the official Christian church, but he deplored the violent attempts to force them into baptism. These feelings led to his decree that the Jews were no longer to be threatened and mistreated. All efforts to convert them to Catholicism were to be peaceful ones. The result: for some five hundred years, though troubled by periodic shows of dislike and at times attacked by individuals and groups, the Jews were allowed to live quietly.

THE MIDDLE AGES

That peace was shattered by Pope Urban II in the Middle Ages, long after the death of the Roman Empire and at a time when the outlines of present-day Europe were beginning to take shape. The trouble started in the eleventh century when the Pope called for the original Jewish homeland, now known as the Holy Land in honor of Christ's birth there, to be recaptured from the infidel (non-Christian) Muslim people who held it. Urban's call launched the wars known as the Crusades, a series of eight major attacks (plus the fruitless and silly Children's Crusade) made on the Holy Land by Christian armies over a period of 176 years. And launched simultaneously was an intense hatred of the Jews.

But why this sudden hatred? Why should the Jews suffer because the Crusaders were at war with the Muslims? The obvious answer, as many historians see it, is that the European Christians, caught up in the frenzy of a newborn war and bursting with hate for a distant foe, took out their anger on a group of people close at hand, a people whom they saw as strange and who, to use the Christian term, were "infidels" just as the Muslims were.

Once triggered, the hate, which was seen first in Germany, spread to all parts of Europe. The Jews found themselves the targets of vicious and absurd stories. The stories depicted Judaism as a bloodthirsty religion and its followers as a cursed people who well deserved to be detested and mistreated. Here are some of the charges that they and their religion endured.

Basically, the Jews were regarded as subhuman creatures who had inherited an assortment of loathsome physical, mental, and moral traits from their forefathers. They were ridiculed for giving off a foul body odor—a hypocritical charge if ever there was one, coming as it did in a time when bathing was little known and little practiced by the population as a whole. They were said to have terrible sores all over their bodies. The rumor went round that Jewish children were born with their right hands attached to their heads, a condition that had to be corrected by surgery.

BLOOD STORIES

The stories about the body sores and the infant surgeries quickly led to the most outrageous charge of all—that the Jews were murderers. Blood, so the charge went, was needed to heal the sores and perform the surgeries. The Jews were accused of killing Christians to obtain the necessary blood.

But the "blood stories" did not stop there. New and even worse ones cropped up. People whispered of how the Jews were committing what were soon being called "ritual murders." The Jews, it was said, were killing male Christian children to secure blood that was then sprinkled over the unleavened bread (matzos) eaten during Passover, a Jewish holiday observed every spring. Further, there were endless rumors of Jews sneaking into Catholic churches and piercing the communion wafers—called hosts—to make them bleed. Many Christians swore that they had actually seen the hosts bleeding.

(Scientists have since established the reason for the "blood" on the hosts. They've found that certain foods of the time—the communion wafers among them—contained a bacteria that, when exposed to the air, showed itself as a red stain.)

Though the tales of ritual murder were born in the Middle Ages, the idea behind them can be traced back to the Bible and the story of the first Passover, which took place in those distant years when Moses and the Jews were held as slaves in Egypt. Moses instructed his people to sprinkle the lintels and side posts of the doors of their homes with the blood of a male lamb. An avenging angel, he said, was coming to slay all the firstborn of Egyptian families. The lamb's blood would point out the Jewish homes and enable the angel to "pass over" them. Now, in the Middle Ages, the anti-Jewish tales substituted the blood of a male Christian child for that of an ancient sacrificial lamb.

Historians point out that all the blood stories were nonsense. On at least two counts, the most vicious of the tales—those about the ritual murders—should be held in special contempt. First, the Jews had opposed the idea of human sacrifice ever since the days of Moses. Second, their dietary laws had long forbidden them to eat the blood of animals.

More than anything else that was ever said about the Jews, the ritual murder stories contributed to the widespread anti-Semitic attitude that the Jews engage in strange religious practices. That attitude persisted for long centuries after the Middle Ages and is still to be seen in many people today. Though the idea that Jews would kill for their religion is no longer taken seriously, the attitude itself is still with us. It exists because of feel-

Sechs Knaben zu Regenspurg von den Juden ermordet.

The most vicious and damaging anti-Semitic libel circulated during the Middle Ages was the charge of ritual murder. This illustration from a medieval anti-Semitic text shows Jews draining the blood from Christian children to use in their religious services.

ings that, if voiced, would say, "The Jews may no longer kill, but I'll bet they're doing *other* odd things for their religion. After all, they've been under suspicion for centuries now." Even in the most modern of times, old ideas die slowly.

We may no longer believe the blood stories, but the people of the Middle Ages certainly did. They were living, remember, in an age of war frenzy. Also, for complex reasons, it was an age rife with superstition, ignorance, and anxiety. The very age itself made such outlandish tales possible and readily believed; and made it possible for them to inspire a fear and hatred that could, and did, erupt in blind panic and attacks on the Jews.

For instance, in the mid-1200s a boy disappeared from a town in England. Instantly the entire country was throbbing with the news that Jews had kidnapped the youngster, crucified him, and drained him of his blood for their Passover bread. The king, wanting to avoid widespread rioting and damage, tried to end the matter by having eighteen Jews arrested and charged with murder. They were then executed after having been tortured into confessing the crime. A short time later the boy's body was found. His blood had not been drained. Nor did he bear any signs of crucifixion.

Sometime later in Germany, a man shocked the people of his city when he swore that he had seen Jews break into a Catholic church and grind the communion hosts to bits. The result: mobs of hysterical townspeople attacked a Jewish neighborhood and murdered a number of its residents.

OTHER TALES

The Bible did more than serve as the basis for the stories of ritual murder. It also served as "proof" for the truth of still other tales. One held that Jewish men grew horns. This idea was grounded, many historians think, in a Biblical description of Moses when he came down from Mount Sinai with the Ten Commandments; it said that his face was "shining." The actual word used was "koran," which could be translated as either "shone" or "horn." Nowadays the accepted translation is the former, but the people of the Middle Ages decided on "horn."

The idea of horns was especially frightening at the time because the Devil, as remains the case today, was usually depicted as a horned creature. Since he was also traditionally pictured as having a tail, the Jews had to suffer the widespread rumor that they, too, had tails. When the great Italian sculptor of the 1500s, Michelangelo, carved a statue of Moses, he topped it off with horns.

All the stories and all the hatred at last resulted in a number of official actions to separate and protect the Christian from the Jew. Social contact with Jews was forbidden in many areas. In Spain, any Christian woman who lived with, married, or had sexual intercourse with a Jew ran the risk of being put to death. The same went for any Christian male who had anything to do with a Jewish woman. And, of course, the death penalty was also imposed on the Jewish partner.

Many countries barred Jews from certain lines of work. Some countries, imitating the Muslims to the east, demanded that their Jewish populations wear identifying marks to separate them from everyone else. In southern Europe a disklike badge, often colored yellow, had to be worn. To the north, distinctively fashioned hats were the order of the day.

Cultural attacks were soon to be seen. The Passion Play, a theatrical presentation that lasted several days and depicted Christ's crucifixion, gained widespread popularity. In it the Jews were portrayed as the cruel and treacherous executioners of Christ. Later, the Jews were to be characterized in much literature as greedy, two-faced, and physically misshapen with hunchbacks.

And, as was seen in the incident of the kidnapped English boy, the hatred triggered much violence. Some of the very worst acts of violence occurred when the first of the Crusaders set out for the Holy Land. Along the way they viciously attacked Jewish villages and urban neighborhoods. Homes were burned, shops pillaged, and livestock stolen. Countless Jews lost their lives.

Though the Christians were responsible for all the trouble, it must in fairness be said that the Catholic Church did not usually give its support to the many hate stories and outbursts of violence. With few exceptions the centuries saw Catholic leaders speak out against what was happening and take steps to safeguard the Jews. One especially noteworthy example of Catholic protection occurred just six months after Pope Urban II called for the freeing of the Holy Land. In the German city of Worms, a band of Crusaders stormed through the Jewish district and killed all but a few of the people living there. Those few saved themselves by submitting to forcible baptism or by taking refuge in the palace of the city's bishop. The bishop gave them sanctuary, kept them safe from the rampaging Crusaders, and then spent the next years protecting any Jew who came seeking his help.

The Crusades were fought over a period of 176 years, but the anti-Semitism that they fostered was to endure among Europeans for centuries to come; in sad truth, right up to our own times. And, as we'll see in coming chapters, the Europeans were to carry it westward in the next centuries when they crossed the Atlantic to settle the New World.

As had been the case since the earliest of times, the anti-Semitism born during the Crusades came principally from religious differences, fears, and misunderstandings. Since then, these same factors have been at fault not only for much anti-Semitism but also for many of the prejudices directed against other peoples. Only in the late nineteenth and then the twentieth century did the world's major faiths—mainly because of the efforts of countless farsighted and sensitive priests, ministers, rabbis, and congregations—begin to work together to achieve a greater understanding and appreciation of each other's beliefs and rights. It is work that continues today at all levels of the faiths.

CHAPTER FOUR

THE BIRTH OF OTHER HATES

Thus far, we've watched anti-Semitism take its first shape and then grow through the centuries until its eruption into full blossom during the Crusades. In discussing the roots of the problem we've come upon the reputation that the Jews won early as good businessmen. We've viewed the suffering that came about because they were fated to live as strangers in foreign countries. And we've traced the conflicts that rose out of their religious beliefs and eventually led to the charge that the Jews engaged in strange, even murderous, religious practices.

But the roots of the problem tell just part of the story. Anti-Semitism, you'll recall, thrives on all the basic ideas that were listed in chapter 1. We covered but a few of those ideas up to this point. Now it's time to see how the rest of them came into being. We'll start with the charge that the Jews are a clannish people.

THE CLANNISH JEW

Along with the charge that the Jews engage in strange religious practices, here is perhaps the oldest of the anti-Semitic ideas. It may even be *the* oldest.

The feeling that the Jews are a clannish people who want little or no traffic with others is grounded in two historical facts. First, as you know, the earliest days of Judaism did indeed see the Jews isolate themselves from their gentile neighbors at the eastern end of the Mediterranean. The Jews did so, in the main, by establishing dietary laws that led them to regard gentile eating habits as dirty. To protect themselves they were soon shunning all dealings with the "unclean" ones. It was a course of action bound to anger and insult the gentiles—and it did. Born right then was the enduring idea that the Jews are clannish.

The second fact can be traced back to the early years of the Diaspora. At that time the Jewish leaders had ample reason to suspect that their people were fated to be wanderers. Twice in the past the Jews had left home, going first to Egypt and then to Babylon. Now, in the wake of Christ's death, Roman overseers had crushed two Jewish rebellions and were threatening to stamp out Judaism, and the Jews were again fleeing, this time in all directions. Facing these facts, the Jewish leaders began to shape their religion in a very significant way. They developed it into what can be called a "portable religion"—one that could be taken along to any spot in the world.

(Many historians believe that the Jewish leaders may have begun to suspect the fate of their people as early as the Babylonian exile and to have begun the shaping at that time.)

Whatever the case may have been, the shaping rendered monotheistic Judaism even more different than it already was from the surrounding pagan religions. The pagan religions were all local in nature. Their gods were local deities—gods of local harvests, local rains, local droughts, local illnesses. The pagan worshipers knew little or nothing of the gods in charge of such matters elsewhere. And the same could be said of the pagan temples and shrines. They were all local, used by local worshipers and dedicated to local gods.

And so, when pagan groups moved from one area to another, or were taken to a distant land as prisoners, they came upon a whole new set of gods, temples, and shrines. Very soon they forgot their old religion and began to worship as the people around them did.

But not the Jews. Their leaders, in developing Judaism into a "portable religion," avoided this problem. They enabled the people to take their God and their beliefs with them wherever

they traveled. Two actions were chiefly responsible for giving Judaism this "portable" quality. Throughout the Babylonian exile, and for years afterward, the leaders put the laws and beliefs of Judaism into writing, inscribing them in a holy book called the Talmud. The Talmud could be easily carried to any country and then, once there, could serve to keep the Jews from forgetting their old beliefs and taking up the religion of their new home. Next, the leaders established the synagogue: the building, or even the room, where the Jews could congregate to worship and to review and discuss the teachings contained in the Talmud. The synagogue could be set up in any place where the Jews settled.

But just what does all this have to do with the charge that the Jews are clannish? The answer is simple. Whenever the Jews first migrated to a new country in the next centuries they settled together and established neighborhoods of their own so that they could pool their manpower and money to build synagogues. Then the Jews who followed settled in those neighborhoods because it was there that the synagogues were located. By doing something for the most understandable of reasons, the Jews continued to leave themselves wide open to the charge that they were clannish.

Then came a development that turned the whole matter into a "vicious circle." As you know, the Jews were first welcomed in many of the countries to which the Diaspora took them. For several centuries they enjoyed a "golden age" in the Arabian countries where the Islamic religion was taking shape. Far to the west those same centuries saw Jewish skills in trade, finance, science, and the arts win a happy greeting in such European countries as Spain, Italy, and Great Britain. The Jews made major contributions to the growth of all these nations and, as they did so, many of their number left their neighborhoods and settled among the general public. But eventually—due to combinations of religious, political, and economic problems—the wel-

An Orthodox rabbi reading the Talmud, the book of Jewish law handed down through the centuries

come was withdrawn and the Jews were struck with discriminatory measures. One such measure was the requirement that they be restricted to living together in their own neighborhoods. Because they were now *forced* to live among themselves, we might think that the idea of clannishness would die out. But it didn't. People too often pass their bigotries from generation to generation, and so a very old and outdated idea refused to die.

It was still alive centuries later during the worldwide emigration to the United States in the late 1800s and early 1900s. (We'll talk more about this migration in chapter 8.) Several million Jews were among those who came seeking a new life in the U.S. On arrival, most settled in Jewish neighborhoods. They did so for the most natural of reasons. The land was alien to them and they wanted the comfort of being near people of their own kind—people who worshiped as they did, spoke as they did, worked as they did, and often came of the same families as they. Countless Germans, Scandinavians, French, Poles, Irish, and Italians did the same thing on arrival. And yet they were not widely accused of clannishness, especially when the coming years saw them, or their offspring, begin to leave their original neighborhoods and blend in with the rest of the population. But the Jews were criticized as clannish—even when they, too, departed their first neighborhoods. Like all bigoted views, it made precious little sense. All that can be done is to repeat that many old ideas *do* refuse to die.

The fact of the matter is that the Jews are probably no more clannish than any other people. A sense of clannishness is a facet of the human personality. Today most of us may not live in neighborhoods made up exclusively or predominantly of our own kind, true. But we all share feelings that are essentially clannish. We are drawn to and feel a kinship with people of our own race or religion. We find that many of our friends are those who share our personal interests. We join social, civic, business, and political groups whose members by no coincidence have interests, backgrounds, and aspirations similar to ours. This being the case, we become—to use an old saying—"the pot calling the kettle black" when we malign one group of people for being what we all are.

Also growing through the centuries was the feeling that their clannishness meant that the Jews thought themselves superior to all others. There is hardly any doubt that the earliest Jews themselves were at fault for this attitude. Their view of the gentiles as unclean *was* snobbish. But, as shown above, there was little or no snobbishness in their later decision to live in their own neighborhoods. Much of the charge that the Jews think themselves a superior group came from the rampant anti-Semitism of the Middle Ages. It was then that bigots happily turned to the biblical story of Abraham telling the ancient Jews that they would be Jehovah's Chosen People, watched over and protected, if they would worship Him and spread His word. Is not a group that looks on itself as the Chosen People a snobbish lot? So went one of the most asked questions of the day.

THE CURSED JEW

One of the worst of all anti-Semitic ideas first took flower at the start of the Crusades. It was an idea based on a statement made in the Gospel of St. Matthew concerning Christ's crucifixion. Although the Roman leaders ordered his death in part, Christ, who was himself a Jew, was executed because his teachings threatened the power of a small but powerful local Jewish faction, so they denounced him as a revolutionary. Matthew wrote that, at the time of the death sentence, some anguished Jews who had sought his freedom moaned, "His blood be upon us, and on our children."

To many a Christian mind of the Middle Ages—and to many a mind ever since—that single statement was all the proof needed to show that the Jews were eternally cursed by God for what they had done to His Son, and that they knew they were cursed. And as proof that the curse was actually at work, Christians pointed out that the Jews were the world's only rootless people. They were forced to roam the world without ever having a country to call their own. What greater curse could there be?

Worse, this idea gave birth to the belief that the Jews deserved whatever mistreatment came their way. Justified in the minds of many people were the falsehoods told about the Jews and the attacks leveled against them as individuals and as a group. Many Christians even thought that their anti-Semitic libels and attacks were willed by and pleasing to an angry God for the loss of His Son. In our own century, Germany's Adolf Hitler revealed this misshapen type of intelligence yet to be alive when he said that, in ridding the world of Jews, he would be doing "God's work."

THE WANDERING JEW

Christian imaginings of a cursed people brought into being one of the most famous of the world's many legends—the legend of the Wandering Jew. Sometime in the thirteenth century the story took shape that Christ had passed a Jew while carrying the cross to Mount Calvary. The Jew taunted Christ with the words, "Go quicker," to which Jesus replied, "I go, but thou shalt wait till I return." Those words doomed the Jew, so the story went, to roam the world until Christ, as Christians believe he will, returns to earth.

The story, as told above, appeared in a pamphlet thought to have been printed in Holland in 1602. The pamphlet reported that a German bishop had met a Jew in 1542. The Jew had given his name as Ahasuerus and had said that he was the man who had taunted Christ. Homeless, he had been wandering the face of the earth ever since.

The pamphlet was widely read in Europe and caused people in a number of countries to imagine that they had seen the Wandering Jew. It was published after the advent of Protestantism and is suspected of having been an early example of Protestant anti-Semitism. The story was most heard in Europe's Protestant countries and little known in the Catholic nations. The legend persisted for centuries. It is not taken seriously today.

Though Christ may not have doomed a Jew to countless years of wandering, the same cannot be said of many of the countries in which the Jews lived. On several occasions these nations forced their Jewish populations into a wandering existence by ordering them to leave. A prime example is Spain in the late fourteenth century A.D.

In the eighth century the Arabs conquered Spain. At the time, as you'll recall from chapter 3, the Jews were enjoying a golden age in the Arabian regions along the North African coast and to the east of the Mediterranean. Many of the Jews traveled to Spain with their Arab friends to take advantage of the economic and cultural opportunities there. Though experiencing anti-Semitic problems now and again, the Jews contributed much to Spanish life for more than six hundred years. They were years that ended with the Arabs surrendering control of the country to the Christians.

The Spanish Christians, unlike their brethren elsewhere, did not at first mistreat the Jews. But then came the year 1391 and the fiery words of a fanatically anti-Semitic priest. He spoke out so vehemently against the "infidel" Jews that everywhere they suffered waves of rioting and killing. To save their lives, many Jews had themselves baptized. Then, pretending to be Christians, they practiced their own religion in secret.

Suspecting them to be Christians in name only, the Spanish state began an investigation of the baptized Jews in 1478—an investigation known as the Inquisition. Its aim was to drag the truth out of them with probing questions and physical torture. In many instances it succeeded in doing so, but it also triggered a Jewish outrage that threw the country into turmoil. The turmoil reached its height in the 1490s, when all the nation's Jews were expelled from Spain. Soon thereafter a number of other regions followed suit. The Jews were ordered to depart Sicily, Sardinia, Portugal, and Italy's kingdom of Naples. Many of the expelled Jews went to Turkey, Greece, Germany, North Africa and other parts of Italy. In most of these places they were welcomed and established thriving communities.

We come now to the last group of basic ideas on which anti-Semitism thrives. They range from the belief that the Jews are a shady business people to the charge that they are loyal only to themselves and to their recently acquired homeland, Israel. It is a trio of ideas that brings us to the subjects of money and power— subjects so broad that they require a chapter of their own.

CHAPTER FIVE

OF MONEY AND POWER

There can be no doubt that many Jews are superb businessmen. Jewish commercial abilities were clearly demonstrated as early as the Babylonian exile. In the centuries of the Diaspora, many of the countries to which the Jews traveled were either in economic difficulty or were trying to develop themselves into economic powers. They welcomed the newcomers for the talent that they could contribute to commercial growth.

A FIRST WELCOME

Three such countries were Italy, France, and Germany. Between A.D. 500 and 800 they invited the Jews in and asked them to help found cities and develop a commercial trade at home and with other nations. In France during the early Middle Ages, a Jewish class of international merchants emerged. Trading with nations as distant as India and China, they imported the Asian spices so popular among the Europeans—and so needed to disguise the taste of foods that always began to rot quickly because of the lack of refrigeration.

England was yet another country that welcomed the Jews. Beginning in the tenth century A.D., Jews established themselves there as bankers and moneylenders. By the 1100s they had become bankers and lenders for most of Europe.

Still another welcoming country was Poland. Seeking to develop its trade in the thirteenth century, it encouraged Jewish immigration. There, royal edicts safeguarded Jewish civil and religious rights.

Far to the southeast, Turkey likewise encouraged Jewish immigration—and for the same reason. Jewish businessmen and artisans were soon playing major roles in the silk-weaving, dyeing, and tanning industries in Turkey and the regions of the nearby Balkan Mountains.

A CHANGE FOR
THE WORSE

But then came a change. As many of the countries—among them France and Italy—gained economic strength, they began wanting their commerce to be handled by their own people. They turned on the alien Jews and edged them away from the center of business life. In England all Jewish business transactions were carefully monitored by the government and then severely taxed. Finally, to be rid of their business influence altogether, England expelled great segments of its Jewish population in 1290. France did the same thing in 1306, 1322, and 1394.

Further, in Poland, the Jews were thought to be on the side of the ruling class in a revolution in the seventeenth century. They suffered attacks and massacres at the hands of the revolutionaries. From then on, Jewish life and commercial activity in Poland deteriorated.

The trouble in Poland and the desire of many countries to place their commerce in the hands of their own people were not the only factors conspiring against the Jewish businessmen. Equally important was the vicious anti-Semitism engendered by the Crusades. In fact, it may have been even *more* important. Many historians feel that the anti-Semitism of the day was chiefly responsible for the still widespread idea that Jews are shady businessmen and not to be trusted in money dealings.

This anti-Semitism did more than cause these countries to remove Jewish businessmen from the center of commercial activity. It also saw the Jews barred from working on or owning land in many countries. Likewise, it saw them barred from earning their living in various jobs and from joining the guilds (the labor unions of the day) which permitted workers to enter certain trades, crafts, and professions. Some wealthy and influential Jews were allowed to continue as bankers. But most businessmen were left no option but to work as shopkeepers, small-scale merchants, and moneylenders.

THE HATED
MONEYLENDER

Though the vast majority of Jews were shopkeepers and modest merchants, it was the common practice of moneylending by individuals that caused the trouble. Today moneylending is a respectable activity carried on by banks, savings and loan institutions, and other financial organizations. But for two basic reasons it was a despised occupation in earlier centuries.

First, moneylenders have always earned their living by charging and collecting interest payments on the funds being loaned. That interest adds up to a percentage of the total money being lent. The amount of interest charged is governed largely by the economic conditions prevailing at the time of the loan. At times it can average as low as 3 to 5 percent. At others it can range up to 15 or 20 percent—or more. Borrowers know that they must pay this interest; simple logic tells them that without it the lender would soon go out of business and there would be no funds available for them. But emotionally, they don't like it—not now or at any time in history. Culturally, the moneylender has always been seen as the coldhearted exploiter of the financially troubled.

Second, moneylending often involves the hated practice of usury. Usury today is defined as the charging of an exorbitant interest on a loan: say 20, 30, or even 50 percent at a time when reputable lenders are charging perhaps 5 or 10 percent. It may also call for the amount of money owed to rise sharply should the borrower fail to repay all or part of the loan on time. The targets of usury are customarily desperate people who cannot

*During the Middle Ages many Jews became moneylenders
after being barred from most other occupations. The
Jews were thus despised and resented for their occupation, which was condemned by the Catholic Church,
in addition to being mistrusted for their religion.
Throughout the medieval period, anti-Jewish riots and
massacres followed the rising tides of anti-Semitism.*

obtain loans from reputable lenders. Perhaps they are too poor to be good risks for repayment. Perhaps they are shady or criminal types. Lenders engaged in usury have long been known as "loan sharks." The term is also often used derisively to mean any moneylender.

In the Middle Ages and for several centuries thereafter, usury did not mean what it does today. It had nothing to do with the charging of exorbitant interest payments. Rather, it was defined as the very act of lending money and charging interest of *any* kind on it.

This definition was established by the Catholic Church in the early years of Christianity. The Church saw moneylending—even though a perfectly legal practice in many Catholic regions—as a major sin because it fed so much on the desperate poor. Catholics were forbidden to function as lenders. At one time, any Catholic who defied this rule was subject to excommunication, that is, subject to dismissal from the Church. The Church did not change its definition of usury to the one presently in use until 1830.

In all, then, the Jews who turned to moneylending because there seemed no other way to make a living could not help but be despised by the gentile public of the Middle Ages and the centuries that followed. They were charging interest payments that, even when fair, were detested. They were chastised for lending money to kings and nobles—money that was then often used to finance local wars. In particular, they were seen as fattening themselves on the poor, people who desperately needed the loans to survive. And, with the Catholic Church so dead set against moneylending, they were regarded as sinners. It was then but a short and angry step to branding them, and all Jews, as shady and unscrupulous businessmen.

There is no argument that Jewish moneylending—whether by individual, bank, or company—*did* bring in vast amounts of money over the centuries. Customers seeking financial help included not only Jews themselves but also non-Jews from virtually every part of the world: gentiles of a practical bent who were able to set aside their anti-Semitism when they needed funds for business or personal use.

For instance, throughout the years following the Columbus voyage of 1492, Jewish banks and companies often financed enterprises for the exploration and settlement of the New World. The same can be said of the ventures that, especially from the 1700s onward, took explorers and business entrepreneurs to other parts of the globe in quest of commercial opportunities. With the coming of the Industrial Age in the early 1800s, Jewish banks and companies in nations that depended on trade—such as Germany, Holland, France, and England (where the Jews had by now returned)—played a significant role in financing the worldwide development of factories and manufacturing processes. One of the largest financial institutions of the day was the international Jewish bank, the House of Rothschild. It was a firm that not only financed commercial ventures but also contributed heavily to cultural and charitable activities.

The huge amounts of money involved in Jewish lending through the centuries helped people everywhere take another step in their thinking—the step to the mistaken belief that most Jews must be rich. And then there was still another step—this one to the suspicion that rich Jews are so greedy that they want to dominate the world. It turned out to be one of the most outlandish and dangerous ideas ever concocted.

WAVES OF HATE

In preparing to talk about this idea we have to spend a few moments with a basic historical fact: Anti-Semitism everywhere is like the ocean surf pounding against a beach. It comes and goes in waves.

At times, the wave of hate—for any combination of religious, political, economic, and social reasons—is massive. At others, again for some combination of the above reasons, the wave recedes, washes away. The dislike still remains to one degree or another. But overall, it is far less intense.

The great wave of hate that rose in the Middle Ages finally subsided in the late 1700s when the idea of democracy swept Europe. After the people of France rebelled against their monarchs in 1789 and established a government based on democratic principles, they granted Jews the rights of full citizenship. Soon thereafter, when French armies under Napoleon moved into Germany and Italy, they removed the gates of the ghettos—the neighborhoods into which the Jews had been jammed—and freed their residents to live wherever they wished.

In England the ghetto system had never been widely used, but Jews had been prevented from rising high on the social scale. Now, in the mid-1800s, Jews were permitted to practice law. Employment in public office was opened to them. In 1858 a Jew, Lionel de Rothschild, won admission as a member of Parliament's House of Commons for the first time in British history. Benjamin Disraeli, another political figure of Jewish descent, served as the nation's prime minister in 1868 and from 1874 to 1880.

In all, the democratic views of the age gave the Jews an improved social, commercial, and political status in western, central, and southern Europe. They were on their way to the positions of citizen equality that they enjoy in most European nations today.

But en route to that equality they experienced fresh waves of anti-Semitism. The trouble was seen principally in central and eastern Europe: in Germany, Austria, Hungary, Russia, Poland, and Romania.

From 1815 onward, for instance, the Jews in Germany and neighboring Austria and Hungary suffered for the new freedoms they were winning. They felt widespread antagonism and heard calls for repressive measures because the surrounding gentiles feared that they were rising too high along the social and economic scale and might one day dominate Germanic life. The fear persisted through the century and saw the birth of the term "anti-Semitism." It was invented, you'll recall from chapter 1, by a German writer named Wilhelm Marr. It appeared for the first time in his pamphlet on the dangers posed for Germany by the Jews.

The worst anti-Semitism was to be found in Russia and her neighbors, Romania and the once-welcoming Poland. It was here, especially in Russia and Poland, that one of the largest Jewish populations in Europe was to be found—some 5 million people in all. Most were confined to an area on the Russian-Polish border known as the Pale of the Settlement.

Russia, an intensely Christian country at the time, had never appreciated the Jews in its midst. They were shunned by the population and suffered government discriminations because they were branded infidels. In fairness it must be said that a few Russian tsars, or rulers, *did* treat them humanely and did try to assimilate them into the general population. Such lenient treatment, however, was not the order of the day in the late nineteenth century.

The problem was that Russia feared the democratic ideals spreading through Europe. She had long been a despotic nation, ruled by her tsars and nobles who let the working and peasant classes endure lives of poverty. But now word of Europe's new thinking was reaching the Russian workers and peasants and causing an increasing unrest among them. There was the ever-present danger of rebellion—a danger that finally became a reality years later when revolution broke out in 1917 and saw the tsar overthrown and the beginnings of today's Communist government established. Frightened by the unrest, the tsars and nobles attempted to deflect attention from themselves by making scapegoats of the Jews, by blaming them for various of the nation's problems.

The tactic worked, at least for a time. There was a Russian version of the era of the Crusades. Hate stories ran riot, telling of how the Jews committed murder for their religion and of how so many of them were secretly rich. Physical attacks on Jews became commonplace. Worse, beginning in the 1880s, the government itself joined in the violence with what were called ''pogroms.'' These were frequent, government-sponsored attacks on Jewish communities. In time, the word pogrom came to mean any attack on a Jewish community, no matter whether triggered by the government or some group of citizens.

These attacks destroyed countless homes and caused much injury and death, not only in Russia but in neighboring Poland and Romania. The pogroms, along with all the other aspects of the anti-Semitism of the times, drove millions of Jews to abandon their homes in eastern Europe and flee to the United States. We'll see this flight in detail in coming chapters.

As if the situation wasn't bad enough already, a new element was suddenly dropped into it during the first years of the twentieth century: the idea that rich Jews wanted to dominate the world.

WORLD DOMINATION

Coming as it did at the start of our own century, the idea of rich Jews seeking world domination is one of the newest of the anti-Semitic attitudes. It centers on a rumor that swept first through Russia, Poland, and Romania and then made its way to the rest of Europe. The rumor had it that a document called the *Protocols of the Elders of Zion* had just been found. The document, so the rumor went, outlined plans by a small international Jewish group to win control of the world.

Today, the document is known to be a forgery, obviously designed to inflame people against the Jews. The belief is that it was first prepared in France and was then taken to Russia. There, in 1905, it was published as part of an anti-Semitic book written by a religious fanatic named Serge Nilus. The book won a wide readership in Russia and then made its way to the rest of Europe. Nilus himself followed the book wherever it went, giving lectures on the *Protocols* and falsely claiming that noted Jewish leaders of the day were involved in the international plot.

The idea behind the *Protocols* seems to have come from a fanciful chapter in a novel of 1868, *To Sedan,* authored by a German anti-Semite who wrote under an English name. The chapter described a secret meeting of the representatives of ancient Jewish tribes. The meeting took place in a graveyard at Prague, Czechoslovakia. There, hidden in the darkness of night, they hatched their plans for world conquest. It all sounds like a bit of nineteenth-century James Bond tomfoolery.

The news of the *Protocols* soon spread from Europe to the rest of the world. The whole idea is no longer taken seriously, and was not taken seriously in a number of countries at the time.

But, as is true of so many other anti-Semitic myths, it remains alive in many minds.

LOYAL TO ISRAEL

The word "Zion" is included in the full title of the *Protocols*. This word brings us to the last of the major anti-Semitic ideas: the feeling that the Jews are more loyal to their recently acquired homeland, Israel, than to the countries in which they live.

Zion is a word with two meanings. First, in the Old Testament, it refers to the ancient citadel of King David on a hill southwest of Jerusalem. Second, it symbolizes all of Jerusalem and the aspirations of the Jewish people over the long centuries since the beginnings of the Diaspora to have a homeland of their own.

As you'll recall from chapter 2, the ancient Jewish homeland at the eastern end of the Mediterranean was under Roman rule in the early years of the Diaspora. It remained a part of the Roman Empire until the empire collapsed in the fifth century A.D. For centuries thereafter, the little country was principally in Arab hands.

The Jewish call for a homeland of their own was heard a number of times during the passing centuries. It was heard again in the late nineteenth and early twentieth centuries. At that time the intense Jewish suffering in eastern Europe prompted two prominent Jews—journalist Theodor Herzl of Austria and scientist Chaim Weizmann, Polish-born—to launch a campaign known as the Zionist movement.

As had never happened before, the Jewish call was now heard. Weizmann, in 1917, convinced the British government to declare that the Jews should be guaranteed "a national home" in Palestine, as their ancient homeland was now called. The British declaration was soon endorsed by an international peace conference at Paris. Britain was given control of Palestine to help the new homeland take shape.

But it was a homeland that did not immediately come into existence. European Jews began to move into the area during the next years, arriving in their greatest number after Hitler took

Palestinian settlers in the early 1900s on the site of present-day Tel Aviv. The call for a Jewish homeland and subsequent establishment of the state of Israel is considered by anti-Semites to be proof that Jews feel no allegiance to their own countries.

power in Germany in the 1930s and began his brutal anti-Semitic persecutions. Throughout all this time, Palestine was principally occupied, as it had been for centuries, by Arabs. They objected strenuously to the flood of newcomers—newcomers who numbered about five hundred thousand by the start of World War II. The war delayed further preparations for the intended country, and the Jews did not have a homeland of their own until 1948, when Palestine at last became the state of Israel. In 1949 Chaim Weizmann was named the country's first president.

Since then Israel has grown into a nation of approximately 4 million people. With that growth has come the charge that Jews over the world—all intensely proud of the new homeland—have become more loyal to Israel than to the countries in which they live. The charge, which we'll discuss at greater length in chapter 10, is heard mainly among people who feel that the Arabs were wrongly deprived of a land that they had occupied for centuries; and among people who dislike the heavy political and financial support that Jews worldwide have given to Israel for its continuing battles with the surrounding Arab nations over land issues.

The Jews themselves view with alarm and anger the charges of limited allegiance to the countries in which they live. They feel that at any time—and especially in the event of some fresh Arab-Israeli trouble—the charges can loose a fearful new wave of anti-Semitism. They add that their loyalties to the nations in which they hold citizenship, either by birth or naturalization, have long proven solid, both in wartime service and peacetime contributions to culture, politics, education, and business. They find insulting any thinking to the contrary. While admitting to a feeling of kinship with and pride for the new Jewish state, Jews insist that this feeling in no way overrides their loyalties to the lands where they live.

We have now come to the twentieth century. It is the century that has given history its single worst example of anti-Semitism. The man responsible for this outrage was the German dictator, Adolf Hitler. The next chapter bears the title by which the Jewish suffering at his hands has long been known—the Holocaust.

CHAPTER SIX

THE HOLOCAUST

Adolf Hitler was thirty years old and a seasoned veteran of World War I when, in 1919, he joined a small political party in southern Germany. The party consisted of a mere six members at the time, and the energetic Hitler, a born politician, quickly took over its command. He christened it the National Socialist German Workers party—a name that was soon abbreviated to the Nazi party—and then slowly built it into the mighty political force that finally carried him to the head of the German government in 1933.

Hitler's rise to power ranks as one of history's ugliest examples of unbridled ruthlessness at work. He early surrounded himself with armies of thugs who intimidated his political enemies and brutally silenced any opposition to his progress. He told the working people that he cared only for their welfare and hated the capitalists who paid them slave wages; all the while, he secretly courted the capitalists and accepted funds from them for his party. At the time he took the reins of government in 1933, Germany was a republic. In a series of deft and lightning-like political moves, he turned the nation into a dictatorship.

JEW HATER

Throughout his ascent to power, Hitler constantly ranted against various groups—among them the Communists and the Jews—calling them dangers to the German state. The Jews in particular felt his wrath. He branded them cowards and shouted that they had avoided military service in the war (a patent lie because national records showed that some one hundred thousand Jews had served in the German army, with twelve thousand dying in the fighting). As was pointed out early in this book, he charged that Jewish capitalists, eager for munitions profits, had been instrumental in starting the war; it was another outright falsehood. And he went on to warn that rich Jews would like nothing better than to take over economic and political control of the country.

In his speeches and then in the atrocities that accompanied his dictatorship, Hitler showed himself to be one of the most, if not *the* most, venomous of anti-Semites ever seen. Where did his seething hatred come from? In his autobiography, *Mein Kampf*, Hitler recalled that he had felt no animosity toward the Jews as a child, saying that he had known hardly a one, and that he had never heard the Jews criticized or even mentioned at home. If *Mein Kampf* is to be believed (and, since Hitler was trying to put himself in the best light possible, much of the book may not be completely honest), the hatred exploded in full blossom during the years when, as a young man, he was trying to earn a living as an artist in Vienna, Austria, a city with a Jewish population of two hundred thousand at the time.

While walking along a street one day he came upon what he described as an "apparition": a thin, dark-faced man wearing a caftan. Hitler said that he had never seen such a strange creature before. He remembered that he had studied the face closely and wondered if the man were a Jew. Quickly he had altered the question to, Is this thing a *man*?

On the basis of that encounter, Hitler said that he had begun a study of the Viennese Jews. He wrote of visiting their neighborhoods and finding the people unclean and foul smelling— strangers, as he put it, to bath water. And, suspecting that he saw prostitutes everywhere, he accused the neighborhoods of being nests of immorality. Then he went on to say that he had expanded his study to take in all Jews. He was soon convinced that they were to blame for all the worst in culture: the worst music, drama, literature, art, and journalism. Before he was done, Hitler was seeing the Jews as a "spiritual pestilence." It was a pestilence, he railed, more terrible than the killer plagues of bygone centuries.

No one knows for certain whether Hitler's anti-Semitism took flower as he claimed in *Mein Kampf* or whether it had been there festering in him since childhood. One of his boyhood friends once said that the bigotry had likely always been present. He recalled seeing Hitler's dislike of the Jews as early as the future dictator's high school years.

No matter when or how it came into being, it was a hatred that was to wreak havoc on all Jews in the years of tragedy now known as the Holocaust.

THE FIRST MOVES

Once he had won full dictatorial powers, Hitler launched a series of government campaigns. Determined to restore Germany as a major military power and thus erase the shame of her defeat in the First World War, he began rebuilding the nation's fighting forces, doing so in secret because Germany, on surrendering, had agreed never again to maintain a large army and air force. Simultaneously he began reviving German industry and agriculture, in part to support the military buildup and in part to bring fresh wealth to the country. And, as was to be expected, he ordered a string of cold-blooded moves against the Jews.

More than his own hatred was behind these moves. In company with it was Hitler's long-held view of the Germans as a superior race; indeed, in his words, a "master race." As he had done while rising to power, he preached that they were descended from the blond and blue-eyed Aryans, a proud, gifted, and strong people who had inhabited Europe and India in ancient times and from whom, so he claimed, had come the world's finest accomplishments in the arts, the sciences, and the law. But, he continued, they had allowed themselves to be weakened by the intermingling of their blood with that of such inferior races as the Slavs and the Jews and had fallen from the heights of old. It was now time for the modern Aryans to right matters by taking control of Germany and fashioning it into the world's greatest nation.

[62]

*In a Berlin hall hung with banners proclaiming
"The Jews are our ruin" and "The Jews are
our disaster," a standing-room-only crowd
gathered to hear Julius Streicher, the Nazis'
most rabid anti-Semite, in 1935.*

But if they were to do this, Hitler argued, the modern Aryans must never again allow themselves to be weakened by their inferiors. At all costs, the inferiors, especially the Jews, must be kept separate from the people of Germany and must be deprived of their influence on the country's economy and culture. His moves against the Jews were intended to do exactly that.

The attack came from many different directions. The Nazi regime outlawed marriages between Germans and Jews. It ordered that Jewish industrial workers be replaced by Germans. In time the government stripped Jewish industrialists of their wealth and made them surrender their factories and businesses into German hands. The Nazis tracked down Jewish musicians and removed them from the nation's symphony orchestras and dance bands; even the playing of music by such Jewish composers as Felix Mendelssohn was forbidden. In literature, books by Jewish authors were banned; the works of psychiatric pioneer Sigmund Freud, poet Heinrich Heine, and scientist Albert Einstein—all of them Jews—were burned. In education, Jews were barred from teaching positions and discouraged from enrolling in the nation's universities.

At the same time, in an all-out effort to mold future generations to his view, Hitler flooded the schools—from kindergartens through the universities—with anti-Semitic teachings and textbooks, all of them designed to demonstrate the superiority of the Germans and the dangers of having anything to do with the Jews. At the university level such instruction was labeled "racial science." In the lower grades the instruction was given in the form of classroom discussions and games. The very youngest grades were also flooded with such storybooks as *Der Gifpilz (The Poisonous Mushroom)*, which was described in chapter I. The Nazis went so far as to allow, and even encourage, German grammar and high school students to taunt and beat the Jewish children in their midst.

Despite such beatings, there was actually very little violence in the early days of the anti-Semitic campaign. Though ruthless and all-powerful, Hitler was sensitive to public opinion. Wanting not to be troubled or stalled by the anger of foreign nations or by an uprising among the many Germans who secretly detested his regime, he tried to appear as if he were running a just and humane government. Further, to help speed Germany's redevelopment, he needed the raw materials and products that came from foreign companies, many of which were owned and operated by Jews. And so he operated quietly, avoiding brutal physical attacks that would trigger a damaging outrage both at home and abroad.

Even many of the harassed German Jews recognized the initial lack of violence and thought the anti-Semitic campaign to be a political maneuver that would soon end. This was a terrible mistake. It doomed countless Jews to remain at home, hoping for the best, while hundreds of thousands of their wiser brethren escaped to the safety of other nations. Hitler allowed the escapees to leave without trouble. He was happy to be rid of them.

As the years went on, however, violence began to play a greater and greater role in Nazi Germany. Concentration camps appeared. Sent to them were Jews and other "enemies of the state." Once there, the prisoners, often beaten and always poorly fed, were forced to work as slaves for the state's farms and factories. Many of the prisoners were broken for life. Many, on being seized and taken from their families, were never seen again.

CRYSTAL NIGHT

One of the worst and earliest examples of open violence took place in 1938. It was triggered by the action of a seventeen-year-old Jew named Hershel Grynszpan. His father had been hauled off to a slave labor camp and, seeking revenge, the boy walked into the German embassy in Paris, yanked out a pistol, and shot the young embassy officer who greeted him. The officer, his body riddled with bullets, died forty-eight hours later.

The shooting occurred on November 7 and sent a wave of outrage coursing through Germany. Still sensitive to world opinion, the Nazi government did not respond to the tragedy by openly taking harsh reprisals against the Jews. Rather, it secretly called for its supporters to "organize and execute" what

would seem to be a series of spontaneous public attacks on Jewish neighborhoods and businesses. Everything was to look as if the common people were so angry that they took the law into their own hands.

As a result, the night of November 9, continuing past midnight, became one of terror for the entire Jewish population. Throughout Germany mobs of Nazi thugs, accompanied by the nation's riffraff, stormed into Jewish neighborhoods. Smashing furniture, breaking windows, and setting fires, they rampaged through synagogues, homes, shops, banks, and offices. Jews were pummeled at home and on the street. Many were shot as they tried to escape the onslaught. Some were trapped and burned to death when their homes were set ablaze.

The violence did several million dollars' worth of damage. Alone, the broken window glass in homes and shops added up to 5 million marks, the equivalent of 1.25 million American dollars at that time. Because of all the shattered glass, the Germans and then the entire world were soon remembering the hours of terror as "Crystal Night"—in German, *Kristallnacht*.

The attack sickened the world and decent people throughout Germany. But worse was yet to come. As soon as he had rebuilt the nation's military might, Hitler, with an eye to dominating all the countries of Europe, launched the series of invasions that ultimately led to World War II. Wherever his forces went, the Jews suffered. In Austria they were savagely beaten and made to clean the streets of Vienna on their hands and knees. In Poland all Jews were rounded up and jammed into city ghetto districts; the Warsaw ghetto, which previously had a population of about 50,000, was choked with as many as 450,000 people. In all the conquered nations, Jews were imprisoned in concentration camps and made to work as slaves for the Nazi regime until they died of mistreatment, exhaustion, or starvation.

The morning after Kristallnacht,
and the beginning of the end for
Germany's thriving Jewish population

Then, in the midst of World War II, came the most barbarous development of all. Begun in 1942 was a program known among its Nazi instigators as "the final solution to the Jewish problem." Its monstrous aim was to exterminate all of Europe's 9 to 10 million Jews.

"THE FINAL SOLUTION"

Though it wasn't originally planned that way, the extermination program consisted of three parts. The first part saw Nazi troops drive trucks into Jewish districts and load them with residents. The residents were fooled into going peaceably by being told that they were being moved to a new area to be "resettled" there. The trucks then made their way to some remote countryside spot where the passengers were ordered out, made to strip, and herded into a great pit. A moment later there was the deadly rattle of machine-gun fire. It continued until not a victim was left standing. When the pit was piled high with corpses—and with some people yet living—it was covered over with dirt and lime. The clothing of the dead, and the gold fillings that were chipped from their teeth after death, were shipped to German cities for sale there.

The Nazis looked on this system of mass murder, which took hundreds of lives at a time, as a highly efficient one. But for a number of reasons—one of which was the difficulty of keeping the giant graves a secret and thus avoiding widespread resistance by Jews marked for death in the future—they soon abandoned it. Phase two of the extermination program was adopted.

It centered on the use of "gas vans": sealed trucks and buses able to carry fifteen to twenty people supposedly bound for "resettlement." Once the doors were closed, the engine was started. Via pipes attached to the vehicle's exhaust system, carbon monoxide poured into the passenger compartment. The passengers suffocated to death in about fifteen minutes.

Like the first system of death, the gas vans were soon abandoned. Doing away with fewer than two dozen people at a time, they were discarded as too inefficient a means of mass murder.

THE WORST OF
THE KILLERS

Now, in the program's third and final phase, the most efficient and horrendous system of all came into use. Gas chambers were built on the grounds of a number of concentration camps. The chambers were concrete, hermetically sealed buildings large enough to hold from two hundred to two thousand camp prisoners. As soon as the victims were herded inside, the doors crashed shut and a lethal gas, hydrogen cyanide, was released through pipes built in the walls. A choking, screaming death for all came in three to fifteen minutes.

The Nazis first tried carbon monoxide in the chambers. But it killed too slowly for their liking, in about twenty-five minutes, and so was soon replaced by the faster-acting hydrogen cyanide.

When prisoners were brought to an extermination camp— the name by which any concentration facility with a gas chamber was soon known—the state of their health was immediately checked. Those found to be strong or in reasonably good health were made to work as slave laborers. The elderly and the ill and weak of all ages were instantly sentenced to the chamber. The strong followed later when they finally weakened or fell ill.

In the first days of the chambers, camp officials made no secret of the fact that execution was at hand. Pandemonium often resulted. Terrified, the prisoners dashed through the camp in a desperate and vain effort to avoid death. Family members clung together, screaming, and tried to fight off the guards. Mothers shielded their children, begging that the little ones be spared, or tried to hide them. The camps solved this problem by keeping the purpose of the chambers a secret and posting them with signs that designated them as bathhouses. Newly arriving victims were then deluded into entering on the pretext that they were going to take showers. One camp, to give its chamber an innocent look, went so far as to surround the place with grass and plantings. Then an orchestra of women prisoners was made to play cheerful tunes while the victims undressed in preparation for their "showers."

Gas chambers were built in approximately ten camps, most of which were located in Germany and Poland. Of all the camps, the largest was to be found just outside the small Polish town of Auschwitz. On its grounds were four chambers. Each could hold two thousand prisoners. Looming nearby were giant ovens in which the bodies of dead victims were cremated. Estimates hold that the Auschwitz chambers took 2 million lives.

No one knows for certain how many Jews—and such other "enemies of the state" as Protestants, Communists, homosexuals, Poles, Czechs, Russians, and gypsies—died in the concentration camps because of the gas chambers and the terrible living conditions. All, really, that can be said is that prior to the Nazi atrocities there were between 9 and 10 million Jews living in Europe. By the end of World War II, in May 1945, more than 6 million of their number were dead.

THE TRUTH AND A CHANGE

Throughout the world people had long heard rumors and reports of the concentration and extermination camps. Now, as the long years of the war came to an end, newsreel cameramen followed the liberating Allied troops into the camps. The horror of what had been going on came fully to light through pictures of filthy barracks, mass graves, gas chambers, blackened ovens, and, most of all, surviving and starving prisoners who looked more like walking skeletons than living human beings.

And coming to light also were other horrors. Surviving prisoners told of how women inmates, often in exchange for food or a clean blanket, had been pressed into service as prostitutes for their guards. They remembered how German guards had peered in the windows of the gas chambers and had laughed as the people within, choking and screaming, had trampled over one another to reach and claw at the great doors. They then went on to detail the insane experiments that Nazi doctors had conducted in the name of medicine.

There were stories of children being battered on the head with clubs to see how much pain they could stand. And there was the story in one camp of a naked prisoner left outside under

A man meditates before the flower-draped crematorium at Auschwitz as another visitor stands in the doorway leading to the gas chamber. Thousands visit the infamous death camp each year to commemorate the millions of Jews who were slaughtered there by the Nazis during World War II.

a sheet throughout a snowy night as guards periodically doused him with cold water—all for the purpose of learning how long the human body could withstand freezing conditions. And there were stories of terrible surgeries performed in sexual and population control studies.

As a result of all that was seen and heard, a sickness and revulsion at what Hitler had done was felt everywhere. The Allied commander-in-chief, U.S. General Dwight D. Eisenhower, on visiting a concentration camp, spoke for decent Germans throughout the world when he said that the sight of the place made him ashamed to be of German descent. Flowing in with his words and the worldwide revulsion came a new and long overdue sympathy for the Jews.

For centuries now the Jews had endured prejudice, discrimination, and persecution in Europe and, in more recent years, in the United States. Their sufferings had reached an intolerable peak in the Holocaust years. Those sufferings—and the fact that so many victims had stubbornly and courageously survived the horror—brought about a great change. The next years were to see the Jews treated with greater understanding and respect. They were years, however, that were to end sadly with a rebirth of anti-Semitism in many quarters.

To tell fully the story of what happened in those years— years that will bring us up to the present—we must go back to an earlier time and look at the history of the Jews in the United States.

CHAPTER SEVEN

THE AMERICAN STORY

THE BEGINNING

T

he story of the Jews in the United States is made up of two contrasting sides.

On the one hand Jews have, without question, been treated more fairly in America than in most nations where they have settled. They have not ever been forced to live in certain neighborhoods (though many did so by choice or economic necessity on first arriving in the U.S.); nor have they ever been required to wear special clothing or pay special taxes. They have not had to face the wholesale deportations once ordered in Spain, Great Britain, and France. They have not endured the pogroms that stained Russian history in the nineteenth century. And, above all, they have never been made to suffer the atrocities met in Hitler's Germany.

Rather, the Jews have been allowed to blend themselves into the social and economic fabric of the U.S. and have been free to live, work, and worship as they please. As a result, they have found a place in every walk of American business and professional life: as shopkeepers and small businessmen, as industrial laborers, technicians, and executives, as doctors, lawyers, teachers, accountants, political leaders, and performers. And, though there remain predominantly Jewish districts in many U.S. cities, Jews have found a place in every American neighborhood, living peacefully alongside those of any faith or ethnic background that can be named.

THE FACTORS OF
GOOD FORTUNE

Jewish good fortune in the United States has been made possible by four factors: (1) the constitutional guarantee of the freedom of worship and speech; (2) the firm American insistence that church and state always remain separated; (3) the fact that the United States has long been a racial and cultural "melting pot" and has made room for newcomers of every color and creed; and (4) the individual American's traditional admiration for anyone who, regardless of backround, achieves success in life, no matter how modest or great that success might be.

Although, as we'll see, Jews have been on the American scene since the earliest days of the nation's settlement, their greatest migration came in the late nineteenth century, a time that also witnessed the arrival of countless gentiles from throughout the world. Most of the Jewish newcomers, in common with their gentile counterparts, were a poor, even poverty-stricken, people in search of the opportunity to prosper and to live, think, and worship freely. That they, again in common with so many of their gentile counterparts, found that opportunity is seen in the fact that in time they and their children pressed out from the slum areas in which they had first settled because they could afford no better. They entered the mainstream of American life to make their mark at all levels of business, professional, and cultural enterprise.

How great a mark did they make? The answer is to be had by listing just a few of their number who achieved outstanding success and made major contributions to the nation. Over the years, the U.S. has benefited from the work of such native-born and naturalized citizens as financier-statesman Bernard Baruch; political leader Abraham Ribicoff; Supreme Court Justices Felix Frankfurter, Louis D. Brandeis, and Benjamin N. Cardozo; scientist Albert Einstein; symphony conductor Leonard Bernstein and concert musicians Artur Rubinstein, Vladimir Horowitz, and Isaac Stern; opera singer Beverly Sills; newspaper executives Adolph S. Ochs (founder of the *New York Times*) and Joseph Pulitzer (founder of the *St. Louis Post-Dispatch* and the Pulitzer prizes for outstanding accomplishments in journalism, music, and literature); playwright Lillian Hellman; radio and television writer Gertrude Berg; motion picture producer Samuel Goldwyn; singer Barbra Streisand, actress Stephanie Zimbalist, and comedian Jack Benny. Golda Meir, prime minister of Israel from 1969 to 1974, was born in Russia, but was raised in the United States.

In all, American Jews have realized such success and have given the country so many contributions that many historians have been reminded of a captivity of centuries ago and have called the American experience a "second Babylon."

But all this is just one side of the story. There is another side—an ugly one—to the Jews' American experience. It sadly reveals that, despite the nation's traditions and constitutional guarantees, the United States has not been without a strong anti-Semitic streak, just as it has not been without its other racial, cultural, and religious bigotries. Ever since the first days of the country's settlement, the Jews have felt the lash of prejudice. Sometimes U.S. anti-Semitism has been slight, sometimes great. Let's now chart its presence through the years.

THE TIME OF DISCOVERY

It is no exaggeration to say that Jews have been on the American scene since the very discovery of the New World.

As proof of this claim, we need only look back to 1492 and Columbus' voyage. When he set sail from Spain to find a westward sea route to the Far East and stumbled instead upon a hitherto unknown land mass, Columbus was armed with excellent maps detailing the shape of Asia. They were maps that came from men recognized as the best cartographers of the day, Spanish Jews. Most likely they were the work of the very best of all, Abraham Cresques and his son Judah. Both were famous throughout Europe as the "map Jews," with Abraham bearing the official title of "Master of Maps and Compasses" to the royal Spanish house of Aragon.

Further, a number of Jews served as members of Columbus's eighty-eight-man crew. Chief among them was Luis de Torres. Speaking both Hebrew and Arabic, de Torres was signed aboard as an interpreter. Columbus felt certain that a landing in the Far East would see his expedition come upon natives who had picked up the two languages from early overland traders from the West, among them the Jews of the Babylonian captivity. De Torres may well have been the first European to address the people of the New World when, on coming ashore at a Caribbean island, he spoke to the natives in Hebrew and Arabic.

The Jewish interpreter enjoys other claims to fame. In *Jews, God and History*, historian Max I. Dimont credits de Torres with being the man who discovered maize and brought it back to Europe, where it became a basic food staple. Dimont also points out that, contrary to popular belief, it was not England's Sir Walter Raleigh who carried tobacco home from the New World and introduced it into Europe. Rather, Dimont gives credit to de Torres and a Christian friend named Roderigo de Jerez.

The first Jews to settle in the New World came exclusively from Spain. This was because Columbus's discovery coincided exactly with the Inquisition that plagued the Jews in Spain and finally saw them expelled from the country in the 1490s. To escape the terrors of the Inquisition, many Jews immediately fled to the New World, going initially to South America, where they prospered as traders and planters. Eventually, however, their Spanish tormenters (and the surrounding Portuguese settlers) made South American life so miserable for them that they began filtering northward to the first settlements in what was to become the United States.

IN A NEW LAND

The very first of their number, a mere handful, arrived at Plymouth Rock on the coast of Massachusetts in 1621, barely a year after the Puritans had rowed ashore there from the *Mayflower*. The newcomers were admitted to and made a part of the infant colony. But as Ernest Volkman remarks in his book on American anti-Semitism, *A Legacy of Hate*, they led an uneasy coexistence with their Puritan neighbors. The Puritans, though they had sailed westward in search of religious freedom, were themselves not above some age-old European bigotries. They thought that the Jews needed nothing better than to be converted to Christianity and looked on them with open contempt as "Christ killers."

Some three decades later, in 1654, a Jewish trader named Asser Levy brought a contingent of twenty-three friends north from South America to the Dutch settlement of New Amsterdam, later to be taken by the British and renamed New York City. On arrival he was met by the Dutch governor Peter Stuyvesant, a man who bore no love for anything Jewish, and was brusquely advised to go elsewhere. Levy ignored the advice and remained. For his part, Stuyvesant immediately dashed off a letter to his Holland-based superiors in the West India Company, the organization that was financing the New Amsterdam venture. He asked their formal permission to expel the intruders.

In the letter, the crusty, one-legged governor said that the Jewish arrivals were repugnant to every one of New Amsterdam's 750 respectable citizens. They were of a "deceitful race," he went on, and were "hateful enemies and blasphemers of the name of Christ." He did not want to "infect and trouble" the colony with their presence. They had to be sent packing.

The letter backfired on Stuyvesant—for two reasons. First, a number of high-ranking West India Company officials were themselves Jews. Second, the company recognized the economic advantages of having experienced Jewish traders in the settlement. Stuyvesant was told to let the newcomers remain.

Their stay proved to be a successful one and can be said to have marked the beginnings of today's large Jewish population in New York City. They did, however, have to put up with Stuyvesant's bad temper from time to time. In the early 1660s, for example, the governor received company orders to attack rival Swedish settlements that were growing up nearby. Immediately, as author Howard Fast relates in his book *The Jews: Story of a People,* Asser Levy and his friends volunteered for service in the planned attack. Stuyvesant replied with a city ordinance that decreed: Jews are unfit to "serve as soldiers, but shall instead pay a monthly contribution for the exemption." Levy, of course, refused to make any such payments. In time, incidents such as these angered many of the fair-minded people of New Amsterdam and earned Stuyvesant a public rebuke from the heads of the West India Company. And, in time, Levy became one of the most respected of America's early settlers.

Stuyvesant's colony fell to the British in 1664. A few years later, as New York City, it was the scene of an anti-Semitic outbreak. For reasons not clear, a mob attacked mourners attending a Jewish funeral.

Despite instances such as these, historians feel that there was actually little anti-Semitism in early-day America, especially when contrasted with what was going on in Europe. For the most part the Spanish Jews, and then the Polish Jews who soon followed them, were permitted to live in peace. They settled principally in Savannah, Georgia; Philadelphia, Pennsylvania; Charleston, South Carolina; Newport, Rhode Island; and, of course, New York City. Actually, they were few in number, totaling altogether between five and ten thousand people by the time of the Revolutionary War in the 1770s. Their number, so some historical estimates hold, may have been as low as twenty-five hundred to thirty-five hundred. If so, Jews accounted for about one-tenth of one percent of the American population of the day.

WHY THE PEACEFUL
SETTLEMENT

Several factors may account for the peaceful settlement. Some historians believe that matters were helped by the presence of so few Jews; in essence, the belief holds that there weren't Jews in sufficient number to remind their gentile neighbors of all the old European prejudices. Such may have been the case, but there are other possibilities that seem as likely.

First, the country was a wilderness; anyone who dared to forge a home in that wilderness assuredly felt a kinship with all others who were struggling to do the same thing. Further, the initial towns and villages lay at the edge of a vast frontier; there seemed to be room enough for *everyone*. Still further, especially out on that frontier, everyone had to depend on everyone else for help when help was needed. In all, it was a situation that, in day-to-day survival, must have made such matters as personal, ethnic, and religious differences seem unimportant.

And, perhaps outweighing all others, there is the fact that life on the frontier was lonely. The people there were eager to see others and were curious about and welcoming of strangers. In *The Jews,* Howard Fast tells of the fur trader who one day hiked into a small Kentucky backwoods village. The settlers gathered around him and, surprised to find that he was a Jew, wondered if he had horns as they had always heard back in Europe. He was a man with a good sense of humor. He invited everyone to rub his head to find out the truth—and then stood there, grinning, as they took him up on the invitation.

When the Revolutionary War broke out, Jews were to be found fighting on either side, as soldiers in the British forces or in George Washington's Continental army. One prominent Jewish businessman, Haym Salomon, was instrumental in raising large sums of money for the revolutionary army.

Though the Jews were allowed to settle peaceably and though they shared in the human rights established by the new United States at the end of the war, a stain of anti-Semitism was nevertheless to be seen in the country. It was not, however, the kind that erupted into physical violence. Rather, it was limited to political and cultural action. For instance, Ernest Volkman, in *A Legacy of Hate,* reports that John Israel, a prominent figure in early Pittsburgh, Pennsylvania, ran into trouble because of his Jewish name. He was not a Jew, but he found it so impossible to convince voters of this fact that he gave up an effort to seek election to a public office.

Volkman also points to one of the first plays written and produced in the young United States. Titled *Algiers: or a Struggle for Freedom,* it featured a Jewish character who cheated gentiles because he believed the teachings of Moses required him to do so.

THE STAIN DEEPENS

The 1800s saw an increasing number of Jews arrive in the United States. In the century between the close of the Revolutionary War and the dawn of the 1880s, the U.S. Jewish population grew to 250,000. The greatest influx began in the late 1840s when countless Jews fled Germany because of the upheavals and oppressions there—problems that were described in chapter 4. By the time of the Civil War, Jews were to be found living, working, and finding success in all areas of the country, from the Atlantic to the Pacific coasts.

The stain of anti-Semitism that had shown itself in the wake of the Revolutionary War deepened in the opening years of the 1800s. Chiefly responsible for its spread were the nation's Anglo-Saxon Protestants. They ranked as political and cultural leaders because the earliest settlers and the Founding Fathers had been predominantly of English stock. They now viewed with alarm the increasing number of Jewish immigrants and the increasingly significant role that the newcomers and the earlier arrivals were playing in the nation's growth. They began to fear that the Jews would soon constitute a political and cultural threat to the country. What they really meant, of course, was a threat to their own Anglo-Saxon, Christian domination.

And so the trouble began. On the political front, a number of states—among them Maryland, New Hampshire, and the two Carolinas—took steps to bar Jews from public office. This was principally done by having the state constitutions require that anyone holding public office believe in the divinity of Jesus, a belief obviously unacceptable to the Jews. Similar steps were taken by some states to keep Catholics out of public office. Eventually all these measures were acknowledged for being what they were—violations of the concept that church and state be always separated—and were either ignored or dropped from the constitutions.

Socially the Jews found themselves treated with contempt and hostility, not only by the Anglo-Saxons but also, as the stain deepened and spread, by those of other races. Increasingly heard were many of the age-old European charges: Jews were a cursed race; they were too sharp to be trusted in business matters; and, in search of blood for their religious practices, they murdered Christians. As had happened in Europe time and again, the charges eventually led to violence. In the 1850s, for instance, a rumor that a Christian had been murdered for his blood swept through New York City. Some five hundred men stormed into a synagogue during services, attacked the congregation, and left the building in ruins.

Culturally the Jews were ridiculed in the literature and theater of the day. Popular plays depicted Jews as sly, greedy pawnbrokers and criminals. Often, as was a leading character in a best-selling novel of the 1840s, *The Quaker City or The Monks of Monk Hall,* they were pictured as deformed, bent forward with humpbacks. The character in *Quaker City* is a forger and a blackmailer. In the course of the book, he commits murder for money.

As bad as it was, the anti-Semitism of the period was tempered by two facts. First, though Protestants were much to blame for the problem, many of their leading figures took action against the unfairnesses shown the Jews. In the 1820s, for example, Maryland state legislator Thomas Kennedy worked energetically to have his fellow legislators accord to Jews the same political privileges enjoyed by Christian Marylanders. He was eventually successful in his efforts. Kennedy was not only a political leader but also a Scottish Presbyterian minister.

One of the greatest Protestant stands on behalf of the Jews was seen in 1840. For months that year, Jewish villages far across the world in Syria were attacked and pillaged because of a charge that the Jews had murdered a Catholic priest for his blood. Word of the Syrian accusation spread to the U.S. and prompted an increase in anti-Semitism in some quarters. A group of Protestant clergymen in Philadelphia came together and strongly condemned the blood-killing charge. Moved by their stand, President Martin Van Buren called for the United States to express its sympathies for the Syrian Jews and even to intervene in the situation in an attempt to bring it to an end. His call stands as one of the earliest actions ever taken by the federal government on behalf of an oppressed minority. Van Buren added that U.S. Jews had produced some of the ''most worthy and patriotic of our citizens.''

The second factor that tempered the anti-Semitism of the day was centered on the public respect earned by individual Jews.

In the midst of all the hostility, a great many individual Jews were much esteemed. They were those who had risen, or were rising, to wealth and power in their work. In effect here was the American trait of admiring someone's personal success while at the same time disliking the ethnic or religious background from which he or she comes.

This admiration was best illustrated by an incident in the 1870s. As part of the anti-Semitic movement, many neighborhoods, social and civic organizations, and hotels had long maintained a policy of excluding Jews. In 1877 the respected and wealthy financier Joseph Seligman arrived at the plush Grand Union Hotel in Saratoga Springs, a fashionable vacation spot for the rich. On attempting to register, Seligman and his family were turned away because of their religion. When word of what had happened found its way into the press, a national scandal resulted, with millions of fair-minded Americans condemning the hotel's discriminatory policy.

With the coming of the Civil War in the 1860s, anti-Semitic feelings were put aside, though there was some talk of Jewish businessmen profiting unduly from the fighting. As had been the case in the Revolutionary War, Jews were to be found serving on both sides. For the first time in U.S. history, at the insistence of President Lincoln, rabbis served as military chaplains. The conflict produced nine Northern and Southern Jewish generals. The man recognized as America's first Jewish statesman, Judah Benjamin, served under Jefferson Davis as Secretary of State for the Confederacy.

But in the years following peace in 1865, Jewish heroism in the war was to be forgotten. A fresh wave of anti-Semitism, far worse than the one already seen, crashed in to flood the nation for decades to come. The wave rose in the late 1880s and was caused by a great westward migration of Jews—a migration so great, indeed, that it could be thought of as a "new Diaspora."

CHAPTER EIGHT

THE AMERICAN STORY

THE GREAT MIGRATION

Give me your tired, your poor,
Your huddled masses yearning to breathe free,
The wretched refuse of your teeming shore.
Send these, the homeless, tempest-tossed, to me:
I lift my lamp beside the golden door.

These words, written by the American-born poet of Spanish-German-Jewish descent Emma Lazarus, are inscribed at the base of the Statue of Liberty. Looming 152 feet (45.6 m) above the waters of New York harbor and carved in the form of a woman holding high the torch of freedom, the statue was a gift to the United States from France in 1886. It symbolized what the young nation had long meant to the world: a place to which ambitious and oppressed people from every point of the compass could come to seek a new and better life.

That countless souls had immigrated to American shores over the years was one of the world's most obvious facts. From the few thousand who had established the earliest settlements, the population had grown to over 3 million people by the end of the Revolutionary War. They were made up of just over 2.5 million from England and Wales; about 250,000 of Scottish and Scots-Irish descent; and some 176,000 Germans, 79,000 Dutch, and 61,000 Irish. All other whites—including French, Italians, and Jews—numbered around 28,000. There were about 750,000 blacks in the country, virtually all of them brought in as slaves or born into slavery.

Between 1790 and the outbreak of the Civil War, the U.S. population multiplied in amazing fashion, jumping from 3 million to about 7.25 million in 1810, then to over 12 million in 1830, and on to 23 million in 1850. By 1860 and the first rumble of Civil War cannon, the figure was up to an amazing 31,443,321. In all, the population kept doubling itself every ten years. This phenomenal increase resulted to a great degree from the arrival of immigrants from Europe. The greatest influx of immigrants came in the 1840s and 1850s, when countless Irish people, fleeing terrible economic and social conditions at home, arrived in search of a new life.

Throughout the years the U.S. Jewish population grew steadily, mounting from the approximate 5,000–10,000 of Revolutionary War days to the 250,000 of the Civil War period. The largest number arrived between 1815 and 1849—in all, about 200,000 souls who were escaping a new outburst of anti-Semitism in Germany, Austria, and Hungary. The Jews, however, especially when their numbers were contrasted with those of the English, Irish, and Germans, continued to make up only a minor segment of the population. But in the late 1870s, the situation changed—and changed drastically. The great migration, the "new Diaspora" began.

THE GREAT MIGRATION

Triggering the vast Jewish move to what was yet called the New World were the political and social upheavals that gripped Europe, especially eastern Europe, in the final decades of the nineteenth century. As you'll recall from chapter 5, the Jews found themselves the targets of hate in Germany and Romania and the victims of Russia's cold-blooded pogroms. There seemed but one way to escape the oppression and bloodshed: depart westward across the Atlantic.

And millions did exactly *that*. In 1878, 125,000 poured into the U.S. from Romania (spelled Rumania at the time). They marked the start of what became an endless procession of European Jews through the immigration buildings on New York's 27-acre (10.9-h) Ellis Island. Immigration officials went on to record such figures as:

- 22,000 in 1881
- 24,000 in 1883
- 30,000 in 1885
- 35,000 in 1890
- 70,000 in 1891
- 60,000 in 1900
- 75,000 in 1903

In 1907 a record 150,000 passed through Ellis Island. The human tide continued to pour in until, by 1914, about 2 million Jews had arrived on U.S. shores. The total rose to over 2.3 million by 1929. Of that total 71 percent came from pogrom-ridden Russia, and 17 percent from Romania. (Today, there are close to 6 million Jews in the United States.)

The Jews did not come alone. Joining them were countless other immigrants: English, Irish, French, Italians, Poles, Scandinavians, Japanese, Hispanics, and Arabs. Together, they helped swell the U.S. population to 75 million by 1900, 91 million by 1910, and 105 million by 1920. By 1930 Americans numbered themselves at more than 122 million. (Today's U.S. population stands at over 226 million).

The great migration ranks as one of the most exciting and noble eras in American history, offering, as it did, a new home and a new life for many of the world's socially and economically oppressed people—indeed, the world's "tempest-tossed."

Bustling Hester Street on New York's Lower East Side, the hub of the Jewish immigrant district in the early 1900s

[88]

But it was also a time of burgeoning trouble. Soon after the flood of humanity began pouring in, various frictions were to be seen rubbing the nation raw.

Newcomers and U.S. citizens alike, especially in the big cities, began to feel keenly the press of that surging humanity. At first, because the U.S. economy was healthy and growing, there were ample jobs for the newcomers, but in a short time people started to worry that the jobs would someday run out and times grow hard. They fretted, too, that housing was becoming increasingly difficult to find. Many complained that they were being forced to leave their homes and move elsewhere for safety and health's sake because slum areas were being bred and choked to capacity all around them—this due to the fact that most of the immigrants, both Jews and gentiles, came penniless and could afford nothing but the worst of housing. Before long, native-born Americans and immigrants who had arrived in earlier years and had by now established themselves, were predicting that the newcomers would overcrowd and spoil the country.

The result was a spreading hostility among great numbers of people. It was an animosity that was mainly seen in a movement called "nativism." The word came from "native." The movement had shown itself to a limited extent during the migration before the Civil War. Now, with the coming of the great migration, it intensified and then grew steadily through the years.

Preached by the native-born and the long-established immigrants—all known as "nativists"—nativism held that the country should be strictly for Americans. It looked on the hordes of newcomers of every stripe with fear. Coming from so many different backgrounds they promised, as predicted, to overwhelm, change, and even destroy the way of life that the nation had built. If given the chance, these foreigners could take everything away from the people already here: jobs, money, housing, land, schools, political power, *everything*. At all costs, they had to be kept from doing so. They had to be kept in their place.

Nativism—and the personal prejudices felt by so many people, newcomers and established Americans alike—reached out to touch every arriving group. Because of it the Jews experienced a new surge of anti-Semitism.

[90]

THE NEW INCREASE

The increasing anti-Semitism showed itself in a number of different ways over the next decades. Early on—even, as you know, before the start of the great migration—some civic organizations, social clubs, restaurants, and hotels began excluding Jews. It was an exclusion that led to a nationwide scandal when financier Joseph Seligman and his family were prohibited in 1877 from registering at the Grand Union Hotel in New York's Saratoga Springs. At the same time the fact came to light that certain professional organizations were barring Jews. The press reported a young lawyer's claim that he was being kept out of the New York Bar Association because he was Jewish.

Right from the beginning the exclusions took in housing, with some landlords refusing to rent to Jews. Then, with the arrival of the 1900s, especially the 1920s, many real estate dealers started the practice of refusing to sell homes in the cities and in the newly developing suburbs to any prospective buyer who, as they put it, was of "Hebrew descent" or of the "Hebrew persuasion." This practice came into being when the offspring of the immigrants started moving up the socioeconomic ladder and, seeking better living conditions, left the poor neighborhoods where their parents and grandparents had originally settled.

By the early 1900s some of the nation's top universities were likewise imposing exclusions. Greatly at fault here was the fact that nativism was much based on the now-aging Anglo-Saxon fear that the Jews might one day constitute a political and cultural threat to the country. It was a threat that seemed especially great were the U.S. to produce a large number of highly educated Jews. Such schools as Princeton, New York University, and Williams College established "quota systems" that limited the number of Jewish students permitted to enroll. In 1922 the president of Harvard called for a quota system for Jews and, at the same time, asked for a rule that would prohibit blacks from living in the school dormitories. To their credit, Harvard's teachers and trustees turned down both measures. A quiet, under-the-table quota system, however, was installed at the university and remained in effect for some years to come.

Even Columbia University in New York City, a school with an extremely large Jewish enrollment, tried a quota system for a time. It took this step after finding itself the butt of an unending string of jokes that referred to it as the "Jew's school."

OLD IDEAS, NEW VOICES

In addition to the exclusions, people in the passing decades listened as many Americans continued to voice the old European myths about the "dangerous Jews." For instance, the now almost ancient claim that the Jews murdered gentiles for religious purposes was as virulently healthy as ever, at times reaping terrifying consequences. In 1928 a four-year-old girl disappeared from a small city in New York State. Immediately there was talk that she had been killed by Jews so that her blood could be used in the Passover bread. The talk turned to mutterings of taking revenge on all the Jews in town. A riot was averted when the child walked out of a wooded area. She was unharmed and had become lost after wandering away from her family.

Another equally antique charge—this one concerning sexual misconduct—went on thriving and at last ended in a tragedy in Atlanta, Georgia. It was a tragedy that Ernest Volkman in *A Legacy of Hate* calls the "worst anti-Semitic incident in American history."

The trouble began in late April 1913 when the raped and murdered body of fourteen-year-old Mary Phagan was found in Atlanta. At the time of her death she had been employed at the factory of the National Pencil Company. Police accused plant foreman Leo Frank of the crime, principally on the grounds that he had been the last person to see her alive. Frank, twenty-nine years old and a Jew, was arrested and given a trial that Volkman calls a "mockery of justice." The foreman's lawyers and the court judge, Volkman alleges, were incompetent. Furthermore, the jury was plagued by mobs who gathered outside the courthouse daily and, with clenched fists upraised, yelled such demands as "Death for the Jew!" and "Hang the Jew!"

Behind the mob demonstrations was a local lawyer-politician named Thomas E. Watson. A fanatical believer in nativism who had once unsuccessfully sought election as U.S. vice president, he hated all blacks and Jews. In whipping the mobs to a frenzy, Watson called Frank a "lecherous Jew" and described him as "a typical young Jewish man of business, who lives for pleasure and *runs after gentile girls.*" That description appeared in an anti-black and anti-Semitic magazine edited by Watson and was followed by the accusation that both black and Jew lusted after gentile women. It was a charge that European bigots had leveled against the Jew for centuries and that American bigots had leveled against the blacks for years.

In the end, Frank was sentenced to death by hanging. But the governor of Georgia, outraged by the unfairness of the trial and Watson's vicious influence on it, commuted the death sentence to life imprisonment, an action that saw him eventually driven out of office by angry voters. As for Frank, he was attacked and wounded by another inmate soon after going to prison. While he was recovering in a nearby hospital, a mob smashed its way into his room. The young Jew was dragged outside and lynched.

(In 1982, almost seventy years after the Phagan murder, Alonzo Mann, a former worker at the pencil factory, gave police a sworn statement in which he said that Frank was innocent of killing the girl. The worker said that the real murderer had been a janitor named Jim Conley.)

STILL MORE VOICES

As bad as he was, Watson was no worse than other bigots who appeared on the scene with the passing years. Beginning in 1915 the nation witnessed a rebirth of the Ku Klux Klan. Originally formed in the southern states immediately following the Civil War, it had started primarily as an anti-black organization. Now, preaching nativism's "America for the Americans," it struck out at any group disliked by its members. In 1923 the Klan's chief, "Imperial Wizard" Hiram Evans, told his seventy-five thousand followers that "Negroes, Catholics, and Jews are the undesirable elements in America." He said that they would never be able to blend into the society and would always be incapable of living up to the standards set by Anglo-Saxons. Then, voicing the old saw that Jews were more loyal to themselves than to the countries in which they lived, he said that, for them, "patriotism as the Anglo-Saxon feels it, is impossible."

The Klan's views were matched by those of such men as Telemachus Timayenis, Protestant minister A. E. Patton, and auto manufacturer Henry Ford. Timayenis won favor among U.S. bigots when, sounding much like a latter-day Hitler, he preached that Jews were "an inferior race" of corrupt blood, malicious hearts, and devious, criminal brains. The Reverend Patton, after a 1912 visit to Ellis Island, came up with this example of blind nativism:

> *For a real American to visit Ellis Island and there look upon the Jewish hordes, ignorant of all true patriotism, filthy, vermin-infested, stealthy, and furtive in manner, too lazy to enter into real labor, too cowardly to face frontier life, too lazy to work as every American farmer has to work, too filthy to adopt ideals of cleanliness from the start, too bigoted to surrender any racial traditions or to absorb any true Americanism, for a real American to see those items of a filthy, greedy, never patriotic stream flowing in to pollute all that has made America as good as she is—is to awaken in his thoughtful mind desires to check and lessen this source of pollution.*

The statement was more than an example of blind nativism. It was simply silly. It denied all the hard facts of Jewish life in the United States: the fact that the Jews were everywhere blending in with the population, the fact that they were working hard and achieving an increasing success in all fields of endeavor, and the fact that they had been among those who had pushed the American frontier westward. Remember those long-ago Kentucky villagers who had gathered curiously about the Jewish fur trader and had good-naturedly been allowed to rub his scalp to see if he had horns? They would have laughed at the Reverend Patton. So would the people of an early Ohio settlement who had fled an Indian attack. They took shelter at a nearby Jewish trading post and remained there until it was safe to return home.

As for Henry Ford, he was perhaps the most influential of the nativists. In 1920 the auto manufacturer used a part of his great fortune to launch a newspaper called the *Dearborn Independent*. Anti-Semitic from its front to back pages, it was sent weekly to some seven hundred thousand readers. In it, Ford charged that the Jews were involved in an international conspiracy to control the world's economy and cultural life. He claimed that they and the Communists were the chief dangers to the welfare of the United States. Ford proudly announced that it was his purpose to rid the country of both.

THE GOVERNMENT MOVES

In part because of nativist outcries and in part because of the difficulties involved in absorbing all the newcomers, the nation finally enacted a series of laws to control the flood of immigrants.

Actually, there were attempts to stem newcomers as early as the 1880s. By that time thousands of Chinese workers had been attracted to the U.S. by the California gold rush and by the transcontinental railroad construction that followed the Civil War. Providing a source of cheap labor, the Chinese were at first welcomed by the railroads. But eventually they were seen as unfair competition to American workers accustomed to higher pay. And so, in 1882, Congress enacted a law banning the immigration of all Chinese laborers. Though originally intended as a temporary measure, the ban was later made permanent. It was not rescinded until China joined the U.S. as an ally against Japan in World War II.

Beginning in the late 1890s, Congress responded to nativist fears with no fewer than thirty-two attempts to pass a law that prohibited entry to any immigrant over sixteen years of age who could not read English or some other language. Congress passed the law four times, only to have it vetoed as unfair by three presidents: once by Grover Cleveland (1897), once by William

Howard Taft (1913), and twice by Woodrow Wilson (1915 and 1917). Congress, however, eventually won out. The measure was enacted over Wilson's 1917 veto and became law.

It was set aside four years later when Congress enacted the Immigration Act of 1921. The Act decreed that henceforth the U.S. would require that newcomers enter under a quota system. In general, the system limited the annual number of immigrants from a country to 3 percent of the total number of people of that nationality residing in the United States at the time of the 1920 census. Three years later Congress stiffened the entry requirements. Admission was reduced to 2 percent and the census year was set back to 1890.

The decision to set the census year at 1890 was seen by many as favoring the English, Irish, Germans, and Scandinavians because, as had long been the case, they represented the major segments of the population in that year. It was seen as discriminating against the Jews and such other peoples as the Russians, Austrians, Italians, and Slavs. Their numbers in the U.S. were still relatively small at the time. The system was viewed as particularly unfair to the Jews. By far, their greatest number had arrived in the years since 1890 and had come in great part from Russia and the Slavic countries. The system remained in effect until 1952 when Congress passed the McCarran-Walter Immigration and Naturalization Law establishing new national quotas.

A NEW DECADE

History repeated itself when the U.S. put aside its anti-Semitism during World War I. Jews were credited with serving loyally and bravely in the armed forces. And it must be said that, despite Henry Ford's rantings that they wanted to control the world's money, the Jews were not blamed for the great economic depression that struck the nation in 1929 and then continued through much of the 1930s. The 1930s, however, brought the American Jew a new kind of trouble. It was a trouble born in Hitler's Germany.

CHAPTER NINE

THE AMERICAN STORY

WAR CLOUDS

The early 1930s saw a weakening of nativism in the United States and consequently an accompanying drop in anti-Semitism. By now, innumerable immigrant families of all backgrounds had blended themselves into the mainstream of American life, causing many a nativist fear of old to dissipate. Furthermore, the nation was caught in the Great Depression. For many people, there simply was not enough time or energy for hating others. They were too busy trying to survive.

But although in decline among the general population, anti-Semitism was still alive in the 1930s. It was not only still alive but as virulent as ever. It was most readily seen in several individuals and organizations.

FATHER CHARLES COUGHLIN

One of the most notorious of the anti-Semitic individuals was Father Charles Coughlin, a Roman Catholic priest. He attained national fame for a long series of weekly radio talks. It was estimated that his broadcasts drew approximately 3 million listeners.

Born in 1891, Father Coughlin was an accomplished and moving preacher who began broadcasting his talks in the early 1930s. At first, he spoke on the general topic of social justice, but soon turned increasingly to anti-Semitic remarks. He was one of the relatively few Americans who held that Jews—in league with the Communists—were to blame for the depression. It was, in his view, part of their plot to take control of the U.S. economy, and then the world economy.

The priest was violently opposed to the administration of Franklin D. Roosevelt, the nation's president from 1933 to 1945. He believed Roosevelt also to be much at fault for the depression (certainly a spurious charge because the depression had begun before Roosevelt took office) and in league with the Jews. As "proof" of the latter charge, he singled out Roosevelt's 1939 appointment of Felix Frankfurter to the U.S. Supreme Court. Frankfurter was the second Jew (the first had been Louis Brandeis, who served from 1916 to 1939) ever named to the Court. Knowing the president and the new justice to be close friends, Coughlin dubbed the appointment "the Jew deal." It was an obvious word play on the title of Roosevelt's program for economic recovery, the New Deal. Coughlin also referred to Justice Frankfurter and his Jewish friends as "Felix and his happy hot dogs."

Father Coughlin did not limit his anti-Semitic views to his broadcasts. They were also to be found in his newspaper, *Social Justice*. When the Jew-hating Hitler came to power in Germany, the priest expressed his admiration for the new dictator. Coughlin's pro-Nazi sympathies remained evident throughout the 1930s and the opening of World War II. At last, in 1942, the Catholic Church, long embarrassed by his pro-Nazi stand, curtailed his activities. The priest disappeared from the national scene. He died in 1979.

THE HATE GROUPS

The 1930s produced anti-Semitic groups that were as virulent as Father Coughlin was as an individual. One was "The Gentile Co-Operative Association of Illinois." Made up of businessmen and merchants fearful of Jewish competition, it published a booklet called the *Gentile Business Directory*. Listed in the booklet were the names of non-Jewish stores and firms, along with urgings not to patronize Jewish businesses.

Next, there was the small group headed by a retired army

general, George Van Horn Moseley. Sure that the Roosevelt administration was taking the country toward socialism or communism, the group plotted to overthrow the government and install a fascist regime. (Fascism is a political philosophy that stands for a centralized government under dictatorial leadership and calls for severe economic and social regimentation, and the forcible suppression of all its opponents.) When the plot was uncovered, Moseley was summoned before a Senate committee to explain himself. While being questioned, he refused to drink the water that had been placed on his table. He was sure that it had been poisoned by Jews.

Then there were the "Silver Shirts." They were a uniformed gang that, inspired by Hitler's anti-Semitism, gave themselves a name similar to that by which his private army of thugs was popularly known—the Brown Shirts. Under the leadership of a man named William Pelley, the Silver Shirts distributed 1 million pieces of anti-Semitic literature each year.

Pelley's silver-shirted outfit was not the only American hate group to take shape when Hitler came to power and inspired anti-Semites everywhere with his campaigns against the Jews. The Un-American Activities Committee of the U.S. House of Representatives later said that at least 135 anti-Semitic organizations had sprung into existence. By and large, most Americans correctly saw them as rising out of the country's lunatic fringe. All nations have their crackpots. Americans knew that they had their fair share.

THE GERMAN-
AMERICAN BUND

The largest of the hate groups was the German-American Bund, which was headed by Fritz Kuhn. It was dedicated to mobilizing

Radio-priest Father Coughlin, whose broadcasts during the 1930s and early 1940s were filled with spurious and sickening anti-Semitic pronouncements.

America's 12 million citizens of German descent into a fighting force loyal to Hitler, a force that would side with him when "the day of deliverance" finally arrived. "The day of deliverance" were leader Kuhn's words and, though their meaning was never fully explained, it seemed obvious that the Bund was looking forward to a Nazi invasion and takeover of the United States.

The Bund was secretly financed by Hitler and used the money efficiently. It distributed tons of pro-Nazi and anti-Semitic literature that was shipped in from Germany. It held numerous public meetings and rallies, using them all as platforms to praise Hitler, to assert the superiority of the Aryan people, and to warn against the dangers of the Jews. Its members tirelessly sought recruits among the people living in German communities. In Bund summer camps young people were given military training for "the day of deliverance." Military training was even seen on the streets and in the backyards of some neighborhoods. The trainees often practiced what they had learned by attacking Jews on the sidewalks or in New York subway cars.

But, as well financed as it was and as diligently as its members worked, the Bund managed to lure only twenty-three thousand of the nation's 12 million Germans to its ranks. Yet it had a look of power and cruelty that frightened thoughtful Americans everywhere, especially when they watched newsreel films of its giant rallies at New York City's Madison Square Garden. On view were crowds who proudly screamed "Heil Hitler," and uniformed guards who, dressed in the style of the Nazi Brown Shirts, clubbed hecklers and threw them out into the street. For many Americans, the country was being given a hard look at what the future could hold were Hitler not stopped.

WAR CLOUDS

But should the United States, so distant from Germany, do anything to stop the dictator?

Americans everywhere were asking this question as the 1930s drew to a close. It was at the core of a great debate that spread across the nation as Hitler unleashed his troops and began his conquest of Europe. Only the most unthinking of people could not see that he was about to plunge Europe into war.

Actually, the question was divided into two parts. Should the U.S. join in the fight against Germany when the war broke out? And even before the war clouds exploded into a storm, should the country send help in the form of money and arms to the nations under attack or obviously on Hitler's list for conquest?

The debate that grew out of those two questions divided the U.S. into two opposing groups. Both were quickly given names by the press. On the one side were the people known as "isolationists," chief among them a large group called the "American Firsters." On the other were the "interventionists."

In the isolationist camp were those who believed that the country should follow the advice given long ago by George Washington in his farewell address to the nation at the close of his presidency: Stay prudently clear of all foreign political upheavals and wars. They argued that the coming war was Europe's affair and that the U.S. should not waste the lives of its young men by joining it. In the meantime, the nation should not risk being drawn into the future conflict by sending aid to any nation endangered by Hitler. In a nutshell, America's safety and welfare—not Europe's—should come first in the eyes of its people.

On the opposite side of the fence were those who felt that the U.S. should intervene, should step in immediately with aid for the endangered nations and then, should war come, join in the fighting. They saw Hitler as a tryant who thirsted after world domination. If he were not resisted now, he would have to be fought later—after he had subjugated all of Europe. Once Europe was in his hands, he would be all the more difficult, perhaps even impossible, to defeat.

The debate was a legitimate one, with valid points of argument on both sides, and it had nothing to do with anti-Semitism. At least, at the start it did not. But soon there was trouble. It was seen in the America First camp.

Causing the trouble were the many hate groups that believed

the Jews to be money-hungry and seeking to control the world's economy. These groups eagerly joined the America First movement because they saw it as the perfect platform from which to broadcast the argument that rich Jews everywhere wanted the approaching conflict for the wealth in war profits it would bring them. That new wealth would take them long steps toward global economic control. On top of all else, the hate groups argued that the interventionists were being urged along by the profit-seeking Jews. These crackpot views shocked the sensible members of the America First camp and the leaders of the movement tried to get rid of the groups. But the anti-Semites hung on. Their message of hate went out to the nation, attracting many listeners and angering just as many others.

THE LINDBERGH INCIDENT

A number of anti-Semitic incidents erupted from the trouble. The worst involved Charles A. Lindbergh, who had been the nation's most beloved hero ever since the 1927 flight that won him the honor of being the first airman ever to solo the Atlantic Ocean. But before we can talk of the incident itself, we need to look at some background facts. To begin, Lindbergh firmly believed that the U.S. should remain out of the coming war. Much of that belief sprang from a 1938 trip that he made to Germany for a look at the Hitler war machine. It was a look that the Nazi leaders happily provided with tours of munitions plants and visits to army and air force installations. Lindbergh returned home with a chilling message: Never fight the Germans. Hitler has made them invincible.

The visit and the message lost Lindbergh much of the respect that he had once enjoyed. Millions of Americans thought that the Germans had deluded the flier—had staged for him a "show" that had exaggerated their military might. Further, costing him still more respect, he had accepted a medal from the Nazis. The interventionists spent some happy months handing out cardboard replicas of the medal. On it were printed the words: "For services rendered to the Third Reich."

On the basis of the visit, Lindbergh threw himself whole-heartedly into the America First cause. He gave numerous press interviews and speeches. In one of those speeches he shocked the nation, chilled the Jewish population, and delighted the hate groups within the America First movement with an anti-Semitic outburst.

The speech was made in September 1941, just three months before Pearl Harbor and almost exactly two years after war had broken out in Europe. At the time, British Prime Minister Winston Churchill, with his country under air attack, was appealing for greater American participation in the war, and President Roosevelt was authorizing war materials for the beleaguered island country. Against this background, Lindbergh accused three groups of trying to push the U.S. into the disaster of war: the British, the Roosevelt administration, and the Jews.

Lindbergh then had a few words especially for the Jews. He said: "Instead of agitating for war, the Jewish groups in this country should be opposing it in every way, for they will be among the first to feel its consequences. A few farsighted Jewish people realize this and stand opposed to intervention. But the majority still do not. . . ."

The words had a frightening ring to them. What did Lindbergh mean when he said that the American Jews would be "among the first to feel" the consequences of a war? Did he mean that they would suffer as all people suffered in wartime? Or was he saying that factions of the American people would turn on them with angry violence? No one could be sure. But whatever his true intent, the words seemed to hold a dark threat.

It was this seeming threat that made the whole Lindbergh incident so frightening for millions of Americans, Jews and gentiles alike. For the first time in U.S. Jewish history, an American version of the European pogrom loomed darkly on the horizon.

Though perhaps the most famous of the lot, Lindbergh was certainly not the only major public figure to stain the America First movement with anti-Semitism. A scandal erupted around U.S. Representative Hamilton Fish of New York when the news broke that he was allowing such groups as the Silver Shirts to use his congressional frank—the free mailing of official letters—when sending out their hate literature. On being asked about the uproar over the violation, he answered that it didn't "bother" him. "There's been too much Jewism going around anyway," he calmly said.

Another political figure, Senator Gerald P. Nye of South Dakota, cooperated with a group of Hitler supporters in mailing out pro-Nazi propaganda. Much of its content was anti-Semitic. The Senator also pointed an accusing finger at Hollywood's motion picture studios and charged that they were responsible for producing films that criticized Germany and urged America's entry into war. Most of the studios, he said, were run by Jews who feared that they would lose the vast European market for their products were Hitler to emerge victorious from the fighting.

DECEMBER 7, 1941

The great debate—with its terrible overtones of anti-Semitism in the America First camp, overtones that appalled so many of the movement's fair-thinking advocates—raged on until Japanese bombers and fighter planes attacked Pearl Harbor on the morning of December 7, 1941. On the following day, President Franklin Roosevelt formally declared war on both Japan and Germany. As had happened before, the U.S. put aside its anti-Semitic feelings as it got down to the work of fighting the war and producing all the materials necessary for the victory that eventually came in 1945. And, as happened before, U.S. Jews— in both the armed forces and industry—played significant roles in achieving that victory.

When peace finally returned, Jews in the United States, and in many places abroad, found themselves in a new era. It was an era of widespread sympathy and understanding. Greatly responsible for it was the sickness felt for what had happened to millions of their brethren in Europe. Also responsible was an appreciation of the role that Jews in the Allied effort had played in winning the war.

And there was yet another all-important factor at work. The

knowledge of the horrors that Nazi Germany had inflicted on the Jews lauched a widespread movement to end the bigotries—and their attendant injustices and cruelties—directed against any ethnic or religious group. The late 1940s marked the beginnings of a U.S. struggle to end racial and religious prejudice and win true equality for everyone. It is a struggle that continues to this day.

Let's see what the years since the 1940s have brought the Jews, and how those years now seem to be ending in a rebirth of anti-Semitism.

CHAPTER TEN

ANTI-SEMITISM TODAY

At the core of the new sympathy felt for the Jews in the immediate postwar period was a deep sorrow—sorrow for the horrors endured and the lives lost at the hands of the Nazis. That sorrow extended itself to yet another sorrow—a shame (or perhaps a sense of guilt) for the injustices done to the Jews throughout history. It was as if the Nazi atrocities had awakened in gentiles everywhere a much-too-long-overdue sense of human kinship with the Jews. There was the terrible realization that Hitler had not murdered 6 million cardboard figures—6 million greedy, crafty, self-superior, hunchbacked, moneylending oddities. He had murdered 6 million *fellow human beings.*

The new sympathy expressed itself on many fronts.

THE CULTURAL FRONT

In the United States and much of Europe, not only anti-Semitism but also prejudice of any sort came under growing attack in the press, in literature, and in the entertainment media. A best-selling novel of the day in the United States was *Gentlemen's Agreement* by Laura Z. Hobson. The book concerned a gentile journalist who was assigned by a magazine to pose as a Jew and then report on the prejudices and discriminations that he encountered. *Gentlemen's Agreement* was made into a motion picture in 1947 and won the Academy Award as the best film of the year.

Another filmed outcry against anti-Semitism in 1947 was *Crossfire*. Nominated along with *Gentlemen's Agreement* for an Academy Award as the year's best picture, it told the story of a vicious ex-serviceman whose psychotic bigotries drove him to beat a middle-aged Jewish businessman to death.

Both these films were part of a Hollywood effort to speak out against prejudices of all types. Because of that overall effort, the postwar years also saw the first of many films on problems between blacks and whites. Among them were *Pinky* (1949), *Home of the Brave* (1949), and *No Way Out* (1950). Later films with racial and Jewish themes included *The Defiant Ones* (1958), *A Raisin in the Sun* (1961), *Guess Who's Coming to Dinner* (1967), and the comedy-drama of the romance between a Jewish widow and a Japanese businessman, *A Majority of One* (1962). One of the strongest of the films with a Jewish theme was *The Pawnbroker* (1965). *Exodus* (1960) and *Cast a Giant Shadow* (1966) dealt with the founding of the Jewish state, Israel.

Prior to the war, Jews and blacks (as well as members of other ethnic groups) had been depicted as stereotypes in most films. The blacks were shuffling, respectful of the whites, and slow of speech; the Jews crafty, always practical, and stingy. The postwar films dealt with them not as stereotypes but as human beings.

For Jews, the moves along the cultural front in the United States saw the nation's long-standing exclusionary measures— the college quota systems and the barring of Jews from certain restaurants, hotels, beaches, neighborhoods, and jobs—begin to disappear. Today, under the various federal and state fair-practice statutes, such exclusionary measures are forbidden by law.

THE RELIGIOUS FRONT

Both the Catholic and Protestant faiths took steps to attack and condemn anti-Semitism. At international meetings held at Amsterdam in the Netherlands (1948) and New Delhi, India (1961),

Protestant leaders denounced the evils of anti-Semitism and expressed a regret for not having acted more strongly on behalf of the Jews during the years of the Hitler regime. Further, in the years immediately following the war, Protestant leaders worldwide gave much support to the founding of the Jewish state, Israel.

Within the Catholic Church, action was taken to improve Catholic-Jewish relations. This action was most evident during the years of Pope John XXIII (1958–1963). For example, the Pope ordered that certain objectionable references to the ancient Jews be removed from the text used in Good Friday services. At the same time he called for changes in the Catholic view of Jews—a view that, dating back to the earliest days of Christianity, regarded them as infidels in need of conversion to the Church.

An improved relationship with and greater understanding of the Jews was not the only goal sought by John XXIII during his stewardship. In what was, and still is, called the "ecumenical movement," the widely admired Pope actively worked for a better Catholic relationship with all religions.

(Though Pope John's work bore much fruit, it must be said that the relationship today between Jews and the Catholic Church is an uneasy one. The unease is caused by two factors. First, the Vatican, in its diplomatic dealings, has not yet officially recognized the state of Israel. Second, Jews everywhere remember that the Church did not speak out against the Nazi persecutions and atrocities. Many Catholics argue that, in great part, the Vatican remained silent out of the fear that any objections to the Holocaust would intensify Hitler's dislike of Germany's Catholics and cause them increased difficulty. This argument is not widely accepted among the Jews, many of whom regard the silence as a modern example of Catholic anti-Semitism which dates back to the Crusades.)

Despite all the cultural and religious steps that were taken in the postwar years, the world was not to be completely free of anti-Semitism, just as it was not to be free of the prejudices and discriminations leveled against other peoples. In many areas Jews continued to be viewed with suspicion and dislike as "outsiders,'' as crafty in business, and as practicing strange religious customs.

Their lot in Soviet Russia, for example, has been particularly difficult. Dictator Joseph Stalin, in the late 1940s, used the Jews as political scapegoats. He blamed them for all the problems facing the nation as the result of the war and went so far as to say that they had caused the Soviet Union to be unprepared for that war. Later, once the state of Israel had been established, the Soviets (though they officially recognized the new country) opposed many of its policies toward the surrounding Arabs. Over the years since the late 1940s, with only a letup now and then, the Soviet government has accused the Jews of causing political and economic problems at home, of plotting for world domination, and of owning all the munitions plants in the ''war-mongering'' United States.

But the Soviet Union has not been alone in causing the Jews difficulty. Trouble has also come from four other groups. In fact, the four are responsible for the greatest amount of anti-Semitism seen between the end of World War II and the present. They are: (1) the Arab nations, (2) segments of the American black population, (3) the neo-Nazis of Europe and elsewhere, and (4) the Klu Klux Klan of the United States.

ANTI-ZIONISM

The enmity between Arabs and Jews is rooted in the founding of the state of Israel in 1948. Actually, the enmity erupted among the Arabs living in Palestine (the region that is now Israel) and in the surrounding countries as soon as the first plans for establishing the new nation were announced in the 1920s. It was a hostility shared by their sympathizers throughout the world and it came to full bloom with the actual birth of the state. The Arabs looked on the creation of Israel as a theft of land that they had occupied for centuries. Adding to their anger was the fact that Israel contained some of the most fertile acreage to be found in the Middle East.

In their rage, the Arab countries unleashed a storm of anti-

Jewish propaganda. They were, however, careful to say that it was not anti-Semitic propaganda, meaning that it was not directed against the Jews as people. Rather, they insisted that it was "anti-Zionist" and, as such, was simply an attack upon the idea of establishing a new and unwanted state in their midst. The term referred to the early modern campaign to establish a Jewish homeland. That campaign, you'll recall from chapter 5, was known as the Zionist movement.

The Arabs certainly had a reason for their anger: they had occupied Palestine for centuries. But there can be little doubt that the term "anti-Zionist" was a semantic nicety meant to keep them from being regarded as bigots. Their outcries, beginning with the very first ones, contained many a recognizable anti-Semitic element.

For instance, the Arabs made good use of the *Protocols of the Elders of Zion,* the forged document that appeared in Europe early in the century and purported to expose a Jewish plot to take over and dominate the world. From the 1920s onward it was printed repeatedly in Arabic and used to convince the people that the move to establish the Israeli state was an obvious Jewish step along the road to world domination.

In the years since Israel's formation, the *Protocols* have continued to be seen. Excerpts from the document have been printed in textbooks used in Arab secondary schools. Arab soldiers have read the document in their military training handbooks.

Arab propaganda has also attacked Israel on other counts. For instance, a very basic claim through the years has been that Israel is a ruthlessly aggressive state.

ARAB-ISRAELI CONFLICTS

This charge stems from the Arab-Israeli conflicts that have marked the decades since Israel's formation. The nation first took shape in 1948 when the United Nations divided Palestine into two states, one for the Arabs and one for the Jews. At the time, Palestine was under British control. As soon as the British and their soldiers withdrew from the area the Palestine Arabs, and troops from other Arab countries, tried to obliterate Israel by force. The Israelis defeated them, capturing and then keeping much of the territory that the UN had given to the Palestinian Arabs. From then until today, there has been an endless struggle over this territory—a struggle that has seen guerrilla fighting, open warfare, political battles, and acts of terrorism.

The first Arab charges of Israeli aggression came at the end of this initial conflict. Later conflicts brought further charges. Egypt, a leading Arab power, nationalized the Suez Canal in 1956 and attempted to damage enemy commerce by blockading the waterway to Israeli shipping; the Israelis responded with an attack that overran strips of land still held by the Palestinian Arabs and reclaimed the use of the Canal. Then came the Six-Day War of 1967 when Israel, in retaliation for border raids from Arab countries as well as military buildups and attacks from these countries, captured Arab lands below its original southern border. When quiet was restored, Israel refused to give back the lands without a formal peace treaty in return. Next, there was the Yom Kippur War of 1973, in which Egypt and Syria tried to regain some of the disputed lands.

In 1978 Israel and Egypt entered an agrement by which Israel returned certain of the captured lands. Though relations between the two enemy nations were much improved by the agreement, the hostilities in the Middle East did not end. In 1978 and again in 1981, Israeli troops invaded southern Lebanon. The invasions, the Israelis claimed, were in retaliation for attacks launched on Israel by Palestinian Arab forces encamped in Lebanon.

All the warfare has kept alive the charge by Arabs and their sympathizers that Israel, even when it is the attacked party, is an aggressive nation. In the wake of the Six-Day War, a new charge was added. It held that the Israelis treated the defeated Arabs with arrogance by refusing to return the lands lost in the fighting. There were further charges that the Israeli troops treated the defeated Arab troops with contempt and cruelty.

As was mentioned earlier, the Arabs have sympathizers the world over. This sympathy has caused trouble for Jews in a number of countries. In the United States, for example, many people have charged that politically influential Jewish groups and individuals are responsible for the support that the federal government has long given Israel—a support that has created many political and economic problems for the U.S. with the Arab states, whose oil production has been of such importance to the nation. U.S. Jews have also been charged with supporting only those national political candidates who are friendly to Israel. Finally, U.S. Jews have been accused of collecting money among themselves and then sending the funds to Israel, where, totally or in part, they can be used to build the new nation's military might.

One point must always be kept in mind about these charges. They are not, in themselves, anti-Semitic. Whether or not they become anti-Semitic depends entirely on who makes them. Suppose that they are made by an Arab sympathizer who opposes the Israeli state but nevertheless bears the Jewish people themselves no ill will. They are then political charges of an anti-Zionist nature rather than anti-Semitic statements. The same holds true when they are made for the same reason by someone who is not necessarily an Arab supporter. They become anti-Semitic only when someone uses them as an excuse to spread his or her personal hate for the Jewish people.

BLACK-JEWISH RELATIONS

At first glance, it may seem odd that black Americans, who have suffered the insult of prejudice for over three centuries, should feel an antagonism for a group that has shared in the same insult—and for a much longer period. But such is the case. This antagonism, though not felt by all blacks, has long been on the national scene.

Strained relations between U.S. blacks and Jews date back to the 1930s when great numbers of blacks were leaving the nation's rural areas in the South and moving to the cities in search of employment. The urban slum districts in which the arriving blacks settled were often neighborhoods where the immigrant Jews had first lived on coming to the United States during the great migration. By the 1930s many of the Jews had moved on to better neighborhoods. But many remained behind to operate stores and other businesses that they had founded. And many who had moved elsewhere still owned apartment buildings in their old neighborhoods.

The result: many blacks paid rent to Jewish landlords for obviously meager and run-down housing. Many—unless they were willing to suffer the inconvenience of traveling outside the neighborhood to shop—had to buy their food and clothing from Jewish merchants. Many blacks earned a little money by running errands for Jewish businessmen, and many worked as domestics for nearby prosperous Jewish familes. A sharp anger was quickly felt as the blacks saw themselves as being exploited by the surrounding Jews.

It was an anger that, in many cases, was justified. Life in any slum area is brutal, and there can be no doubt that some Jews did exploit the blacks by renting them disgraceful living space and then doing nothing to improve it; and no doubt some Jewish merchants did charge them unfairly for inferior food and clothing. During World War II the anger caused several black newspapers to comment that Hitler was doing everyone a favor by putting the Jews "in their place." The anger has persisted in many black slum areas to this day.

Outside such areas, however, U.S. black-Jewish relations were good in the 1950s. Those were the years that witnessed the nationwide movement for black civil rights: for equal voting, educational, and social rights. It was a campaign in which many Jews, who had experienced their own suffering at the hands of prejudice, eagerly participated. Working for such organizations as the National Association for the Advancement of Colored People (NAACP), they gave both money and time to the civil rights movement.

At first, black leaders welcomed the Jews to the movement, as they did other sympathetic people. Black, Jew, and gentile worked side by side. Early on, Jews went to court with cases challenging the traditions and laws that made school segregation possible. They joined the civil rights workers who fought and marched for equal voting and educational rights in Mississippi and Alabama during the 1950s and 1960s. Two Jews were among the civil rights workers murdered in Mississippi in 1964.

But the late 1960s brought a significant change. The leadership of the movement's various organizations began to be taken over by what the press was soon calling "black nationalists" and "black militants." Among them were such figures as Roy Innis of the Congress of Racial Equality (CORE), Stokely Carmichael and H. Rap Brown of the Student Non-Violent Coordinating Committee (SNCC), and Charles X. Kenyatta of the Mau Mau black nationalist group. The new leaders—militant, enraged over years of humiliation at white hands, and wanting nothing whatsoever to do with those hands—altered the direction of the movement. Scorning its former leaders as "Uncle Toms" for cooperating with the whites, they swung the movement away from its original goals. They turned it into a drive to mold the U.S. black population into a faction separate from the rest of the country's people. It was to be a faction second-to-none in economic, social, and political power. The new leaders introduced into the language a term frightening to countless white Americans of the late 1960s and early 70s: black power.

Black-Jewish cooperation in the movement came to a sudden end. Though angry at all whites, the new black leaders reserved a special attack for the Jews. They saw the Jews as the chief representatives of all that was evil in the white treatment of the black. They were the greedy landlords who charged outrageous rents for ramshackle housing that they refused to repair. They were the shopkeepers who sold poor grades of meat and even spoiled food to their black customers. They were the homeowners who had black domestics sweep up after them for wages so low that they were hardly wages at all.

The charges shocked the Jews and the earlier civil rights leaders. But the Jews really should not have been surprised. What was happening now had happened before in other times and other countries. The new black leadership was making the Jew the scapegoat for all that was wrong with black life in the United States.

The age-old charge that the Jews thought themselves superior was also heard. Throughout the preceding years, Jewish intellectuals had advised civil rights groups on plans and activities. The intellectuals had also been very vocal in describing black problems and theorizing on what could be done about them. The new leaders resented the advice and comments, finding them all signs of a Jewish sense of self-importance. They said that the Jewish intellectuals had taken on themselves the job of telling everyone what it was like to be black in America, and this was sheer arrogance; that job could be handled by just one person— a black. They added that the all-wise Jews had so pushed themselves to center stage in the civil rights movement that the old leadership would not make a single plan without first consulting them.

And there was a brand-new charge. A great many Jews had entered the teaching profession over the years. A number of the new black leaders noted that black children were often not as successful in their schoolwork as the youngsters of other ethnic backgrounds. They accused the Jews of dominating the U.S. educational system and of deliberately overlooking their black students and giving them an inferior education. Why? As one black group—New York City's Afro-American Teachers Association—saw it, the Jewish teachers were engaged in a plot to keep the blacks from getting ahead later in life and competing with Jews on the job market.

Were Jewish teachers actually involved in such a plot? It seems unlikely. There were other, more plausible explanations for the poor showing made by many black students. They included the lack of tax money in ghetto districts for the support of the schools there; the inferior skills of many teachers of *various* ethnic backgrounds; and the fact that many ghetto students thought themselves so doomed to lifetimes of poverty that an education didn't seem worth trying for.

The views of the new black power leadership unleashed widespread anti-Semitism among U.S. blacks. The depth of their hatred was clearly seen in the series of anti-white riots that swept through the nation's big-city black ghettos in 1967. Often the targets of destruction during the rioting were Jewish-owned apartment houses and business establishments. The riots led President Lyndon B. Johnson to appoint the Kerner Commission to study possible solutions for the nation's racial problems.

Black anti-Semitism deepened when the new leaders, thinking that their cause had a greater chance for success if it worked in tandem with other oppressed peoples, aligned themselves with the Third World movements. This strategy linked the black power movement with the Arabs in opposing the state of Israel. The blacks now joined the many Americans who accused the Jews of being behind the U.S. government's long-standing sympathy for and support of Israel.

In time, the black power movement failed. All but a few of the nation's blacks turned away from it and sought other methods of improving their status. The movement's passing was greeted with relief by the many blacks who had felt that its aim of separating them from the rest of their countrymen and molding them into a power bloc would eventually win them nothing. All along they had felt that their race could win a full place for itself in U.S. society only by working with rather than separating themselves from their fellow races in the country.

Today, the black power movement is still alive, but it is no longer the powerful force that it once was. It is seen in such bodies as the Nation of Islam movement, with a membership estimated at ten thousand. The movement is headed by Louis Farrakhan, who has praised Hitler as a "great man" and has called Israel "an outlaw nation." He has predicted that the United States will be torn by a race war in 1986.

THE NEO-NAZIS

The term "neo-Nazism" means the "new" or "recent" Nazism. It is a movement made up of admirers of Hitler and all that he stood for. Universally regarded as manned by society's lunatic fringe, neo-Nazism took shape in secret immediately after World War II and was, of course, made up of people who had supported or worked for the German dictator. Since then it has gathered followers—reportedly only a few at first, but now on the increase—in various parts of the world. Most neo-Nazism today is found in Germany, France, Great Britain, and the United States.

The father of U.S. neo-Nazism was George Lincoln Rockwell, a frustrated magazine illustrator (not to be confused with the famous illustrator Norman Rockwell). Long a Hitler admirer and Jew hater, Rockwell formed the American Nazi Party in 1958. Then, in the next years, he and his small band of followers alternately shocked and amused the nation with their anti-Semitic silliness. They picketed the White House during President Eisenhower's term and brandished signs reading: "Save Ike from the Kikes." Rockwell used a Jewish prayer shawl for a doormat at his party headquarters. He gave endless anti-Semitic speeches and mailed out a steady flow of hate literature, much of it pornographic in content.

In 1962 Rockwell attempted to establish an international Nazi movement under his command. He went to London, met with a small group of neo-Nazis from several countries, formed what he called the World Union of National Socialists, and had himself elected as its "World Leader." The British press contemptuously dismissed the whole affair, with one newspaper sporting the headline: "The New 'World Fuhrer'—Elected by 27 Idiots."

The international movement got nowhere in the next years and Rockwell was killed by a rebellious follower in 1967. Under subsequent leadership, the American Nazi Party struggled on for a time and then seemed to go out of business. The world thought itself rid of the crackpot phenomenon known as neo-Nazism.

But no. Neo-Nazism has suddenly reappeared in the 1980s. It has either been reborn or has come out of hiding. One way or the other, it is back on the scene and is to be found in the several countries already mentioned.

In his book, *A Legacy of Hate,* Ernest Volkman reports that, in the early 1980s, the U.S. Nazi movement grew to a hard-core membership of two thousand. Another four thousand to five thousand people, though not active members, were known to be sympathetic to the cause. Rather than being under a single banner, as it had been in Rockwell's day, the movement now boasted thirteen different groups. They are groups that continue to work today, putting the emphasis of their activities on the wide distribution of pro-Nazi and anti-Jewish literature.

The Simon Wiesenthal Center, a national organization that monitors and speaks out against anti-Semitic activities, recently reported on the most dangerous of today's neo-Nazi groups. It lists among them the Aryan Nations, an organization with known branches in twelve states and headquartered in Idaho. Also named is the National Socialist Party of America. This outfit works out of headquarters in the Midwest, and boasts chapters in thirty-three cities across the country. The party publishes a biweekly newspaper and, according to the Wiesenthal Center, distributes thousands of pro-Nazi booklets and pamphlets throughout the world.

The Center also points to the National States Rights Party, which is based in Georgia. The party is said to have strong ties with neo-Nazi and racist groups in England, West Germany, Belgium, and South Africa. Its publication, *The Thunderbolt,* is distributed underground in these countries.

Worldwide, the neo-Nazis are said to be few in number. Though their main emphasis has been on the distribution of propaganda literature, they are recognized as fanatics who have been turning increasingly to violence in recent times. The Wiesenthal Center reports the following violent acts that have marred the opening of the 1980s in both Europe and the United States.

1. Synagogues in London, Munich, Rome, and Paris have been bombed.

2. Swastikas and anti-Semitic slogans have been painted on Jewish homes, business establishments, synagogues, and tombstones in such countries as England, France, and Germany. Similar actions were commonplace in Germany during the Hitler era. The painted defilements, the Center reports, are now more frequently seen than at any time since the end of World War II.

3. In Vienna, Austria, the home of Simon Wiesenthal has been bombed. Wiesenthal is the famed humanitarian and Nazi hunter whose work is continued by the Wiesenthal Center in the U.S.

4. The National Front, a neo-Nazi group in England, boasts uniformed members who have attacked Jews on the street. They have fought the police when attempts have been made to stop the attacks.

Two women were killed and ninety-five other people injured when a car bomb exploded in the Jewish district of Antwerp, Belgium, in 1981. This is one of many incidents portending a rising wave of anti-Semitism around the world.

5. In the United States, neo-Nazis have been convicted of fire bombing a southern California synagogue. A Chicago Nazi murdered an elderly Jewish man by forcing him to inhale cyanide gas, the lethal gas that was once used in Hitler's extermination camps; the killer then took his own life by inhaling the cyanide. Federal agents in New Orleans seized a large cache of weapons belonging to a neo-Nazi band and the Ku Klux Klan. The weapons were to be used by the two bands in a planned invasion of Dominica, a small island in the Caribbean Sea.

The passing years have also seen other acts of violence by neo-Nazi groups and members. In New Rochelle, New York, an allegedly crazed Nazi shot and killed five people before taking his life with the gun. John Hinckley, Jr., the disturbed young man who attempted to assassinate President Ronald Reagan in 1981, was once a member of the National Socialist Party of America. Police in Louisville, Kentucky, recently stopped a plot by a California neo-Nazi group to assassinate 106 prominent citizens in their city, most of whom were Jews. In mid-1984, a nineteen-year-old neo-Nazi in France told police that he had stabbed a seventy-five-year-old woman to death. Why? For no other reason than that she was a Jew.

THE KU KLUX KLAN

As indicated by the above report of the planned invasion of Dominica, U.S. neo-Nazi groups have recently joined forces with the Ku Klux Klan in order to gain greater strength.

The Klan, you'll recall from chapter 9, emerged from the southern states and became a dominant anti-Semitic force nationally during the turbulent 1930s. Its power diminished with the coming of World War II and for many years was thought to

*Neo-Nazis and KKK members
holding a "Hitlerfest" in
North Carolina in 1980*

be pretty much out of business. But it suddenly bloomed again in the late 1970s and has grown steadily since then, spreading out once more from its southern birthplace to upward of twenty states. Current estimates hold that the Klan now has more than twelve thousand regular members and some fifteen thousand "affiliated" members in an assortment of Klan-like groups.

As it did in the 1930s, the Klan today is responsible for the publication and distribution of material damning any group that it doesn't like, a principal target, of course, being the Jews. It is also responsible for much violence. For instance, in *A Legacy of Hate,* Ernest Volkman reports that the early 1980s saw such incidents as:

1. "In Evansville, Indiana, two Klansmen spray-painted swastikas and slogans ('Death to Jew Dogs!') on tombstones in a local cemetery. One of the men vandalized a synagogue and wrecked a Jewish delicatessen.

2. "In Ada, Oklahoma, a cross was burned near the town and signs exhorted the townspeople to 'stop the Jew anti-Christ.' Klansmen also distributed anti-Semitic literature to local schoolchildren.

3. "In Nashville, Tennessee, three members of the Confederate Vigilante Knights of the Ku Klux Klan were arrested on charges of planning to bomb a synagogue and several Jewish-owned businesses.

4. "In Catonsville, Maryland, a Klansman was arrested as he was about to bomb a local synagogue."

As if recent violence were not enough, greater future trouble is promised by the marriage of the Klan and the neo-Nazi groups. They are known to operate more than six paramilitary camps in several states, among them North Carolina and Texas. At these camps they are preparing their trainees against the day when, as they are deeply convinced, such enemies as the Jews, blacks, or Communists seek to take control of the country. Together, they are growing, spreading themselves throughout the nation, and calling for vicious action wherever they go; the U.S. Department of Justice has reported that, in one recent year, crimes by the Klan and neo-Nazi groups jumped 200 percent and involved acts ranging from arson to murder. And together, the two groups are distributing millions of pieces of anti-Semitic literature to all parts of the world.

It is a literature that seems to be taking effect in various areas. Klan and neo-Nazi organizations have appeared in Canada, Great Britain, and France. In Germany the Klan has been trying to join itself with the large neo-Nazi movement already at work there.

A NEW AND TERRIBLE WAVE

In light of the growth of the Klan and the neo-Nazi groups, there can be little doubt that we are witnessing a new and rising tide of anti-Semitism in the United States and Europe. If so, it could, when joined with the anti-Semitism long felt in the Arab countries and their sympathizer nations, develop into a terrible wave of hate.

The Jews have faced such awful waves of anti-Semitism throughout history—it seems unthinkable that yet another could be building. But what can an individual, regardless of race, color, or religious belief, do to calm any future wave?

There are but two answers. First, knowing of the suffering it has brought, people everywhere must speak out against anti-Semitism, to put an end to the anguish, fear, horror, and injustice endured by countless human beings over a span of almost four thousand years. One person has only a small voice in a vast world. But it is a voice that can have a great and valuable effect if it convinces other voices that they, too, must speak out.

The second answer brings us in a full circle back to the opening pages in this book. We must carefully guard ourselves against anyone who would have us hate a Jew or any other fellow human being. We know the wellsprings of prejudice: the failure to put aside the fears and angers that we feel toward a people because of the things that others have said about them, and the failure to get to know personally the people against whom a prejudice is directed. We need always to make our own decisions, need always to insist that we meet and get to know the hated ones—and then let our fears and angers, as surely they will, evaporate in the friendship and understanding that, just as surely, will come.

FURTHER READING

If you are interested in learning more about anti-Semitism, you will find the following books and magazine articles to be especially interesting and helpful.

BOOKS

Abrahams, Israel. *Jewish Life in the Middle Ages.* New York: Meridian, 1958.

Dimont, Max I. *Jews, God and History.* New York: Simon & Schuster, 1962.

Fast, Howard. *The Jews: Story of a People.* New York: Dell, 1968.

Friedman, Lee M. *Pilgrims in a New Land.* New York: Farrar, Straus, & Giroux, 1948.

Gilbert, Rabbi Arthur. *A Jew in Christian America.* New York: Sheed & Ward, 1966.

Hitler, Adolf. *Mein Kampf.* Boston: Houghton Mifflin, 1943.

Laffont, Robert. *The Illustrated History of Europe.* New York: Doubleday & Co., 1960.

Morais, Vamberto. *A Short History of Anti-Semitism.* New York: W. W. Norton, 1976.

Parkes, James. *An Enemy of the People: Anti-Semitism.* New York: New American Library, 1946.

————. *A History of Palestine from 135 A.D. to Modern Times.* New York: Oxford University Press, 1949.

Quinley, Harold F. and Charles Y. Glock. *Anti-Semitism in America.* New York: Free Press, 1979.

Selznick, Gertrude and Stephen Steinberg. *The Tenacity of Prejudice: Anti-Semitism in Contemporary America.* New York: Harper & Row, 1969.

Shirer, William L. *The Rise and Fall of the Third Reich.* New York: Simon & Schuster, 1960.

Tenenbaum, Joseph. *Race and Reich.* New York: Twayne, 1956.

Toland, John. *Adolf Hitler.* 2 vols. New York: Doubleday & Co., 1976.

Volkman, Ernest. *A Legacy of Hate: Anti-Semitism in America.* New York: Franklin Watts, 1982.

Wirth, Louis. *The Ghetto.* Chicago: University of Chicago Press, 1928; Phoenix, 1956.

Wise, William. *Albert Einstein: Citizen of the World.* New York: Farrar Straus & Giroux, 1960.

MAGAZINES
AND
NEWSPAPERS

Diamond, S. "Jewish State, State of Jewishness," *Nation,* July 23–30, 1983.

Goleman, D. "Anti-Semitism: A Prejudice That Takes Many Guises." *New York Times,* September 4, 1984.

Katz, J. "Misreadings of Anti-Semitism." *Commentary,* July, 1983.

New Republic. "Jackson and the Jews." March 19, 1984.

Time. "Worst Fears." October 3, 1983.

Von Kuehnelt-Leddihn, E. "Jews, Christians and Gentiles." *National Review,* October 14, 1983.

Wisse, R. "Blaming Israel." *Commentary,* February, 1984.

INDEX